Eating Alfresco

THE BEST STREET FOOD IN THE WORLD

Eating Alfresco

THE BEST STREET FOOD IN THE WORLD

Photographs by
NELLI SHEFFER

Text by
ISRAEL AHARONI

HARRY N. ABRAMS, INC.,
PUBLISHERS

EDITOR: *Adele Westbrook*
DESIGNER: *Darilyn Lowe Carnes*

Library of Congress Cataloging-in-Publication Data

Sheffer, Nelli.
    Eating alfresco : the best street food in the world /
photographs by Nelli Sheffer ; text by Israel Aharoni.
        p.   cm.
    Includes bibliographical references and index.
    ISBN 0–8109–2900–7 (pbk.)
    1. Cookery, International.   2. Outdoor cookery.
I. Aharoni, Yiśra 'el.   II. Title.
TX725.A1S4417   1999
641.59—dc21   98–30702

Identifications of front and back cover illustrations, as
well as illustrations on pages 1, 2–3, and 4–5 are to be
found on page 142.

NELLI SHEFFER'S photographs have been featured in
more than forty books on food, as well as in countless
newspapers and journals. His most recent book is
Food Markets of the World, with text by Mimi
Sheraton.

ISRAEL AHARONI, author of nine best-selling food
books in Hebrew, is considered one of Israel's premier
chefs. He is the owner of six restaurants, including the
prestigious Golden Apple in Tel Aviv, and has worked
with some of the world's finest chefs.

Photographs copyright © 1999 Nelli Sheffer
Text copyright © 1999 Israel Aharoni

Printed and bound in Hong Kong

 Harry N. Abrams, Inc.
100 Fifth Avenue
New York, N.Y. 10011
www.abramsbooks.com

Contents

Introduction   7

China   12

France   24

Holland   32

India   40

Indonesia   54

Italy   64

Mexico   74

Morocco   80

Peru   92

Thailand   98

The United States of America   108

Uzbekistan   116

Recipes   130

Acknowledgments   141

Bibliography   142

Index   143

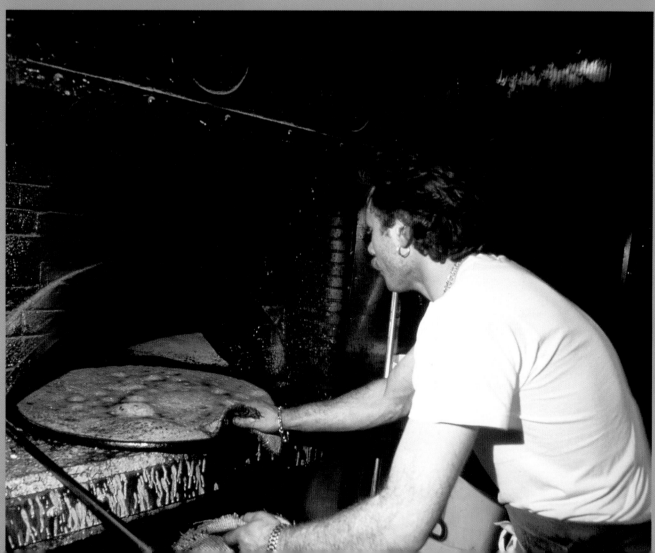

Introduction

Succulent herring and chopped onions served in a fresh bun are a choice street food in the Dutch city of Delft.

Opposite above:
Hot and spicy dumplings being prepared on the street in China.

Opposite below:
A special treat in Nice is the *soka*, a savory pancake of ground chickpeas, popular in the South of France.

*N*elli Sheffer and I have traveled together throughout the world in an unending quest for tasty and interesting things to eat, writing and photographing as we go. During our travels, we have discovered that "street food," which can be found everywhere, is a fascinating genre that involves its own kind of raw materials, its own preparation techniques, and its own style of consumption. Street food can also offer a unique view of the culture, tradition, and folklore of a particular society, as well as a taste of each country's social, religious, and economic realities.

The dynamics of street food are compelling. The social and cultural context, the rainbow of colors and gamut of flavors, the cacophony of voices and the down-to-earth atmosphere provide an added dimension to the eating experience through a direct and unimpeded contact with both vendors and other diners. The often enjoyed scene of arms extended across stalls, hands rapidly exchanging food and money, is one I relish. On-the-spot-cooking invites the customer to share in the experience, to witness the technique, and to become a vital partner in the process. Above all, street food can spontaneously satisfy a sudden urge, an insatiable hunger.

Unfortunately, the idea of street food can strike fear in the hearts—and stomachs—of even experienced travelers. They will often look longingly, but hesitate to partake because of an understandable concern for

Skewers of pork *saté* are readied near a small temple on Bali in Indonesia.

health and hygiene. It goes without saying that it is never safe to eat blindly at just any food stall. Choosing the most promising ones requires a good pair of eyes, a good nose, and more than a pinch of common sense. Does the food look fresh and bright? Is the stall itself reasonably clean? Does the cooking oil smell fresh? Do the stall and its surroundings make a good general impression? If so, this may be sufficiently encouraging for even the most fervent follower of the maxim, "Let the buyer beware!" Upon reflection, the stall's exposure can be advantageous, since it allows one to inspect the "kitchen" and the food before and while it is being prepared, something "established" restaurants don't usually permit.

Street food has a number of attractive qualities. At its best, it is authentic, dynamic, diverse, and a reflection of a country's individual "flavor." Above all, good street food is very tasty. The food products involved are generally local and accessible, suited to the climate and the season. The preparation itself is immediate, ensuring the potential for maximum enjoyment. Throughout the world, street food is put to the test every day and only stalls that exist in dynamic harmony with their surroundings can survive for long.

Most often, people tend to learn about a new place through its history, its art, its architecture, and its natural environment. Eating on the street is another way—a very appealing way—to become familiar with a city or a country. The more you discover about the varied delights of street food, the more you will realize how richly layered and diverse this subject really is, beginning with the origin of a dish, its cultural and culinary evolution, and its relationship to other dishes in the same region or country, and even in other countries.

The link between street food and more formally presented dishes tends to be reciprocal. Sometimes, simple street food evolves into a more elaborate dish that makes its way into the home or the restaurant. On the other hand, sometimes the opposite happens—a fancy dish will shed its royal garb and find its way to the street.

Food stalls can be well established or obviously improvised. Sometimes they are mobile, mounted on wheels or human shoulders, and sometimes completely stationary. During holidays, festivals, and special events, food stalls will suddenly multiply, offering special foods to suit a particular occasion. As one tours

Left:
Thinly sliced *porchetta,* a Northern Italian specialty, will be served on toasted bread.

Below:
A woman from the Atlas Mountains prepares bread in one of many traditional Moroccan ways of breadmaking.

A taco stall. Fresh tortillas with a savory filling are sold on almost every corner in Mexico City.

Left:
In Peru, *chicharrón* are chunks of pork fried with garlic in their own fat.

Below:
A noodle stand window on a Bangkok street in Thailand.

Opposite above:
In the New York borough of Brooklyn, a decorated Coney Island food stand offers the passerby an extensive selection.

Opposite below:
Shorpa, a fragrant and spicy lamb soup, is sold in the Tashkent market in Uzbekistan.

the globe, eating on the street can provide a menu of delicious and diverse dishes.

This book invites everyone to join in a unique culinary adventure. It reflects a personal trek I have made over the years, moving among food stalls throughout the world. There are places I have not yet seen but hope to visit in the future, while there are other places to which I return again and again. I hope the journey through this book will transport the reader—visually, sensually, emotionally, and intellectually—to distant regions, and that a modicum of the magical atmosphere of each spot will be communicated through the words and images that fill these pages. Admittedly, nothing can replace the experience of actually being there (wherever "there" is), so when you arrive at your destination, my advice is to plunge right in—take part in life's feast and enjoy to the fullest the earthy pleasures of the world's best street food.

China

Chong, a pyramid of rice and other ingredients wrapped in bamboo leaves, is a traditional Chinese street food.

*O*ne of the most popular and traditional street foods in China is a pyramid of sticky rice filled with various ingredients, including black mushrooms, which is wrapped in bamboo leaves and tied with a string. *Chong* is the name of this popular steamed dish and vendors pile them high on their carts and serve them from their street stalls. Customers remove the string, open the leaf, and pour hot sauce over the rice pyramid before swallowing it with great gusto.

This rice pyramid dates back hundreds of years to the tale of a despairing prince who threw himself into a river. The fable relates how *chong* were prepared for the fish to eat, in order to keep them from consuming the body of the beloved prince.

Chong represent only one of a dazzling variety of street foods found in China, a country unique in its culinary diversity. For the Chinese, eating out is not so much for diversion or entertainment, but instead represents an integral part of their daily routine. Most Chinese people work very hard and women take their place alongside men as family breadwinners. It is not uncommon, for instance, to see women construction workers balancing themselves on bamboo scaffolding. Their homes are often small, and while most have modest cooking facilities, stopping for something to eat at one of the many outdoor food markets that are open day and night is more convenient. The food is usually excellent and the price is reasonable. One of the best indications of the importance of food in Chinese life is the greeting exchanged in the morning, which can be loosely translated as: "Have you eaten yet?"

Just wandering through China's food markets is a delight. The array of dishes is vast: Noodles in all shapes and sizes; doughy delights crisp and brown or rotund and fluffy, steamed, fried, or baked, stuffed with meat or vegetables of almost every kind; fresh fruit, sliced and aesthetically presented; and many varieties of sweets.

The stalls are arranged in rows, each displaying a different dish, but never more than one or two. Entire days can be spent watching the activity in the market, inhaling the aromas, and sampling the tempting food. Some stalls even have stools and a table or two in front where people can sit down and eat.

Certain dishes, such as noodle soup, really should be eaten sitting down. These soups come in countless varieties and they all offer a treat to the palate. Large empty bowls adorn the tables until moments before mealtime, when the vendor spoons into each one a few drops of sesame oil, fresh bean sprouts, thinly sliced green onions, and some kind of vegetable, generally a leafy green such as bok choy or mustard greens. As soon as the lunch crowd begins to arrive, he throws a handful of noodles into each bowl and pours some hot clear broth over them. Golden drops of sesame oil float to the surface as the vendor adds strips of cooked meat, duck, chicken, shrimp, or other ingredients—in accordance with his experience and inclination—and the hungry crowd is served.

In this small restaurant, bowls will be filled with steaming noodle soup at lunchtime.

These soups are refreshing and satisfying with a surprise in almost every spoonful. The hot broth, the flavor-enhanced noodles, and the other tastes and textures combine wonderfully in the bowl. Around the table, young and old, singles, couples, and entire families sip the broth and slurp the long noodles. This is one of China's most familiar scenes and it characterizes the country no less than sights such as the Great Wall or the Forbidden City.

In general, the Chinese eat noodles in great quantities and not just in their soup. Some noodles are boiled, others are fried quickly in oil, or deep-fried until crisp. The ingredients are simple: flour and eggs, flour and water, rice, soybeans, or mung beans.

A young girl prepares to enjoy her rice noodle soup.

15

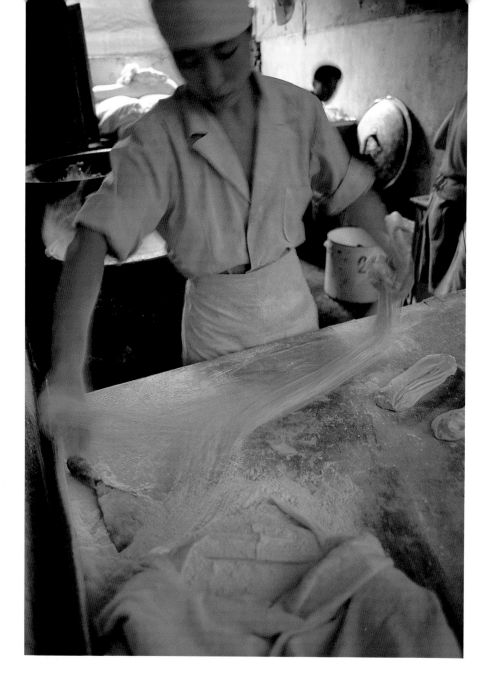

Swift and highly skilled
movements are required to
create handmade noodles.

The preparation process is fascinating. At one market, we saw a vendor making noodles by hand. He stood at the dark edge of his stall holding a slab of dough that he alternately lassoed over his head and beat on the wooden table with quick, smooth strokes. When the dough was sufficiently elastic, he shaped it into a long thin loaf and—clutching one end in each hand—stretched it as far as his open arms could reach. Then he folded that long thick noodle dough in half and once more stretched out the edges, repeating the process several times. Each time, the dough became thinner and the number of noodles he clutched doubled. The speed and skill with which he worked were dizzying and, at one point, it became almost impossible to follow his motions. In less than a minute, he had created a bundle of long thin noodles uniform in width, all by hand, without using a machine or even a knife. With the steam billowing from a pot in front of him, the vendor looked like a wizard before his cauldron. When the noodles were ready, he tossed them into the boiling water with perfect ease and moved on to another task.

In the city of Xi'an, vendors prepare their noodles differently. They begin with a thick loaf of dough that resembles unbaked bread. When an order is placed for noodle soup, the vendor flips a cleaver in even strokes, shaving off tiny bits of dough right into a pot of boiling water, where they cook quickly.

According to Western conventional wisdom, bread is a scarce commodity in China. This may be true if you are looking for the Western version, but the Chinese have their own kind of bread, and they have a selection of baked goods that is second to none in the world.

One of the most bustling and colorful markets in China is located in Xi'an. The food in this nocturnal market is as interesting as it is spicy. Among the varied delights is a type of stuffed bread that the vendor makes in front of your eyes. He tears off a piece of dough from the large unbaked loaf sitting on the counter and shapes it into a small flat circle that he tosses onto an aluminum surface that rests on burning coals. A few minutes later he flips the dough, which by now looks like a round piece of bread with a pocket in the center. As the bread cooks, he throws slices of garlic, ginger, chili peppers, and sliced onions all together into

a hot wok. Smoke rises as the food begins to sizzle. The vendor shakes the wok, flipping the food with well-timed motions, and then adds strips of marbled lamb, spices, and rich black soy sauce. He shakes the wok again and smoothly flips its contents into the prepared pocket of the bread.

In the Yunnan area, another type of bread, known as a *baba,* is popular. Here, too, the vendor throws a portion of round flat dough stuffed with Chinese chives onto an aluminum surface that rests on hot coals. But that's only the beginning. The Chinese have a certain practicality that manifests itself even here, on the street. While the bottom of the dough slowly turns brown, the vendor places another grid filled with charcoal on top of

Baba, a bread filled with green onions, is baked on both the top and bottom.

it, so that the bread cooks evenly on both sides. And, as if that weren't enough, the vendor balances a pot on top of the grid where he prepares tea that can be enjoyed with the meal.

The *bao zi* is the most common type of breadstuff in China. This is a dumpling that can be found on almost every street corner, made with yeast and filled with various delights, depending upon the region. Each dumpling is about the size of a small fist, with the dough gathered at the top in a decorative pattern. These dumplings are steamed in a bamboo dish for about ten to fifteen minutes, and they emerge snowy white and with a distinctive texture unlike any "bread" found in the West.

There are many types of *bao zi*. Some are steamed; others are steamed and then fried on the bottom, making them both fluffy and crispy. The dough in some types of *bao zi* may be thick and chewy, while others are thin and delicate. Some are stuffed, others are stamped with wishes for "Long Life" or "Double Joy." There is a special type that is molded into the shape of a peach with a pink top and green leafy dough on the sides. Since the peach is a sign of long life, these dumplings are often served at weddings.

The most popular "bread" in China is composed of a double line of long thin dough that looks like two sausages resting side by side. This dough is fried until it becomes crispy on the outside while remaining soft and airy inside. It is often eaten at breakfast with *congee*—a kind of rice porridge that may be served with garnishes of meat, poultry, and pickled vegetables.

One of the more delectable sights in China's food markets is a collection of poultry stalls. Their glass tops resemble aquariums in which the various birds hang upside down on hooks: chickens, ducks, doves, quail, and other fowl (including some birds the size of a pinky). Some of the birds have been grilled. They hang brown and shiny, dripping oil. Some are cooked in a red, soy-based sauce, while others are prepared in a white, aromatic sauce. The birds can be bought whole or by the piece, and they may be eaten alone or as part of a more substantial meal.

Residents of Kunming, the capital of Yunnan Province, are enthusiastic consumers of poultry. One of the most common dishes is a Yunnan-style steamed chicken that you see on nearly every street corner. The dishes in which it cooks are its trademark: brown ceramic bowls (some adorned with delicate designs) stacked one on top of the other,

Opposite above:
Preparing *bao zi* that are soft and fluffy on the top, while the bottom is brown and crispy.

Opposite below:
Two kinds of *bao zi* are served from a small window on a Shanghai street.

A stall of roasted chickens and ducks in Kunming offers a tempting display.

billowing steam and an irresistible aroma. The bowls are filled with a thick broth, pieces of chicken, wild mushrooms (abundant in this region), and ginger. They are stacked on a very hot surface, and the heat rises through the little chimneys built into each bowl (a tube that begins at the bottom of the bowl and rises almost to its top). This way, the chicken cooks slowly and thoroughly. The taste is more than worth the wait. Also common in this region is the Yunnan duck, a street version of the royal Beijing duck.

The Szechwan region is also known for its elaborate and diverse cuisine. One of the more popular street foods there is a Chinese version of Western fondue, known as *khwo*. This is eaten at low tables next to a stall, each provided with a bowl full of spicy brown liquid that rests on a hole in the center of the table. There are large trays alongside the tables, filled with bamboo skewers laced with pieces of meat, chicken, fish balls, wild mushrooms, quail eggs, sausages, and various vegetables.

The fun begins when the crowd arrives. As everyone chooses among the skewers, the vendor turns up the heat underneath the bowls until the thick liquid—laden with melted fat and well spiced—begins to bubble. The people sitting around the table then dip their skewers into the boiling liquid, twisting and turning them until the meat and vegetables are cooked to their satisfaction. Even the novice learns quickly how

Above:
On every street corner in Yunnan Province, one sees traditional pots of steamed Yunnan-style chicken.

Right:
Yunnan duck is the popular street version of the royal Beijing duck.

One of the most popular street foods in China:
a Szechwan hot pot.

long to leave the skewers in the boiling liquid, and which combination of ingredients may be the best.

The Western concept of dessert is almost entirely absent from the Chinese tradition of dining. The whole meal, in itself, reflects the Chinese Yin-Yang principle, in which there is harmony between contrasting elements. Sweet tastes coexist with other flavors in such combinations as sweet-and-sour and sweet-and-spicy, and the quest for sweet sensations is satisfied during the meal, not afterward. But on the street, sweets abound: a row of tiny Chinese apples spiked on bamboo skewers and covered with crispy caramel; fruit, fried in a golden batter and topped (like the apples) with a thick, sweet caramel; fried doughy balls sprinkled with sesame seeds and known as "laughing cookies" because of a crack that appears during the frying that looks like a happy smiling mouth. Other snacks to satisfy a Westerner's sweet tooth? How about bowls full of red, black, and green beans, cooked and sugarcoated? There are also tiny, colorful pieces of gelatin covered with a sweet syrup or nestled next to pieces of hand-shaved ice to create a chilled dessert, which is the closest thing in China to Western ice cream.

Dried snacks that can be eaten almost any time are also very popular in China: thin pieces of dried meat in a startling array of flavors and colors, some coated with honey, others so spicy that one bite brings tears to your eyes. There is also a form of dried squid that looks as if it has been run over by a steamroller. The squid is grilled over charcoal and chewed slowly (it takes patience, but it's well worth the effort). For those too old to sustain such chewing any longer, the dried squid is run through a double-wheel with "teeth" that pierce it and gives it a softer texture.

The streets of China offer an amazing array of foods, some familiar to a Westerner, others completely foreign. But most street food in China is delicious, and enjoying its variety gives the visitor a rare opportunity to experience an essential element of Chinese culture, and to engage in a direct encounter with something both exotic and ancient. If there is anything in China that remains alive, dynamic, and authentic, that links the past with the present, it is certainly to be found in the street food that has remained a well-rooted and constant element in a continually changing world.

A vendor offers sugared apples on bamboo sticks in Beijing.

France

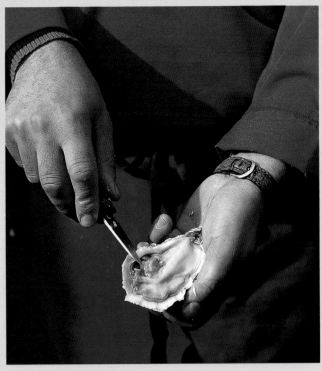

The oyster vendor skillfully inserts his knife and, with one swift movement, opens the shell.

Opposite:
A case of fresh oysters on display outside an oyster bar in Paris.

Some of the best oysters in the world can be found in the fishing town of Cancale, in Brittany, on France's west coast. This picturesque little port lies nestled in a tiny bay. When the tide is high, the fishing boats rock quietly in the water. At low tide, however, the same boats can find themselves beached on the wet, sandy bottom.

That is when the oyster beds can be seen, stretching out along the edge of the bay. The oystermen wade out in their high, waterproof boots to gather the oysters and pack them in boxes for shipment to eager diners around the world. But first, even before the oysters are refrigerated, comes the opportunity for local residents to eat their fill. These delicate, almost transparent bivalves that taste like a concentration of the sea, are served with great fanfare in restaurants and at stalls all along the streets of Cancale. In one skillful motion, oyster shells are split open and the delicious mollusks are served; the happy customer relishes as many as his or her sense of discretion will allow.

Shellfish vendors can be spotted throughout Paris as well, at stalls located near outdoor diners at cafes and bistros. Rich platters of seafood are arranged on a bed of crushed ice, awaiting the pleasure of both customers passing by and those dining at the nearby tables. The variety is dazzling.

Brittany is also home to the crêpe, probably the best known of France's street foods. The intoxicating aroma as the vendor spreads the thin batter over a black griddle to produce that most delicate, large, but paper-thin pancake is enough to encourage even the most reluctant diner, and the choices of fillings seem endless. As the crêpe comes off the griddle, it is immediately filled with butter and sugar, or lemon and sugar, or chocolate, or various jellies and jams, folded into four sections and served warm. Lately, vendors have begun to add trendier fillings, such as butterscotch or peanut butter.

Those are the sweet variety. Savory, mouth-watering versions, known as *galettes,* are made with buckwheat flour and filled with eggs, mushrooms, tomatoes, or ham and cheese. Less delicate than the sweet crêpe, these appetizing versions can easily serve as a quick lunch or late afternoon snack.

Perhaps the most popular street food in France, however, is the sandwich, which the French have elevated to a sublime gastronomic experience. Street stalls throughout Paris sell baguettes filled with the finest cheeses,

In this window are a number of sauces used to sweeten a crêpe.

ham, sausages, pâtés, and almost every other imaginable delicacy. Freshly made and wrapped with a wisp of paper, they are snatched up almost as quickly as they are made. Charcuteries all over town also offer take-out sandwiches for consumption outdoors. Here, the choice is even wider, including terrines, a wide variety of pâtés, smoked meats, roast beef, chicken, pork, several kinds of cooked greens, such as spinach and Swiss chard, and a staggering variety of cheeses. Each day, an Alsacienne charcuterie in Paris sets up a flowered cart outside its shop, stocked with Alsacienne sandwich specialties.

Outdoor lunchtime diners have the banks and bridges of the Seine, or the wide and open squares and parks, such as the Jardin de Luxem-

An inviting sandwich cart on the Rue de Buci in Paris.

The baguette is a French cultural symbol. In the Latin
Quarter, a young student has no trouble eating as she walks.

A couple relishing their lunch outdoors on the Pont Neuf.

bourg or the Jardin des Tuileries, where they can linger relaxedly as they enjoy their alfresco meals. You may see a well-tailored businessman on a park bench, absentmindedly brushing crumbs from his lap as he reads his newspaper and finishes his well-filled baguette. Elsewhere, youngsters in the park feed the birds with leftover crumbs from their own baguettes.

In the Latin Quarter, Tunisian, Moroccan, and Greek-style sandwiches are all the rage. Skewered lamb roasts on a vertical grill, fat dripping down into a pan below. At a customer's request, the vendor will shave off several slices, inserting them into a pita pocket, adding some slices of onion, fresh tomato, and a final sprinkle of parsley. He wraps the pita to form a large cone, and *voilà:* a savory meal ready to enjoy

Grilled Greek sandwiches are made to order in Paris.

29

while strolling down the Rue de la Harpe or watching the *Bateau Mouche* glide by along the Seine.

For those interested in an outdoor dessert, beautifully crafted ice cream carts are part of the Paris scene throughout the year, especially in the Tuileries and other parks. In the fall, as the leaves begin to change color, the chestnut vendors appear, and the heady aroma of roasting chestnuts fills the air.

As one ends an evening in Paris, the street stalls—especially those selling seafood—are still open for business. The temptation to stop and indulge in an oyster or a sea urchin or two, served on the spot, sprinkled with a few drops of lemon juice, is almost overwhelming. Judging by the enduring popularity of these street foods (in particular), many Parisians—as well as many visitors—are regular, and regularly satisfied, customers.

Opposite above:
Food and drink are offered everywhere along the small side streets of the Left Bank.

Opposite below:
Even in the winter, ice cream is enjoyed in the Jardin du Carrousel in front of the Louvre.

Below:
Grilled chestnuts for sale in the Jardin des Tuileries.

Holland

Fried potatoes can be enjoyed in many ways, with a customer's choice of sauces.

Opposite above:
Stubbe, located on a bridge over the Singel canal in Amsterdam, is one of that city's most famous herring stands.

Opposite below:
Assorted small sandwiches and fish snacks make a tempting display.

*M*ore people eat street food in Holland than in most other European countries. Whenever I think of street food in Holland, I think, above all, of raw herring. The herring, that is, which is sold fresh along the canals and on street corners in Amsterdam, deboned but intact, during the season, to be slipped down the throat headfirst, followed by a good shot of *jenever,* the national gin drink made from juniper berries.

Herring season begins the last week of May, when fishermen leave the port of Scheveningen for their first expedition of the year, after having observed a ban against fishing of several months' duration to maintain the level of the fish population. The first barrel of herring traditionally goes directly to the Queen Mother. The second is unloaded on the shore and auctioned off as "first fruits," herring by herring, with the very high proceeds going to charity. These first herrings are considered the best—as the season wanes, the prices go down.

A whole herring slipped down the throat is only one way to enjoy it. Another is in a sandwich on a soft, fluffy roll called a *broodjes.* Here, the herring is not only boned, but also smothered in finely chopped onions and sour pickles.

The weather in Amsterdam can be erratic, and covered herring stalls provide shelter, as well as the opportunity to indulge in a tasty snack. Herring is not the only street food option, however. Smoked eels are

Eating fried potatoes on one of the many bridges in Amsterdam.

another favorite, pressed together on a tray, with the skins already removed. Select one, and the vendor will bone the eel and present it to you in the same *broodjes* used for herring sandwiches. There are also shrimp, steamed mussels, and crabmeat—all served with rich mayonnaise in the ubiquitous *broodjes.*

Patat frites, freshly fried potatoes, are another popular street food in Holland, and they are often sold at their own stands. The potatoes are

sliced, deep fried, scooped up into a paper cone, and served with a choice of mayonnaise or *saté* sauce (a peanut-based condiment that came to Holland from Indonesia).

All sorts of street foods are available in Amsterdam's central plaza, Dam Square, when the square turns into an amusement park. Traditional amusement park foods offered there include cotton candy, as well as hot dogs fried with onions and stuffed into a roll. One hot dog vendor

Cotton candy is popular all over the world, and Amsterdam is no exception.

Buns filled with thinly sliced and sautéed pork, or a juicy sausage, can be taken away to be eaten elsewhere.

may also sell fried smoked bacon and ham, served in the same way. Other vendors sell steak tartare sandwiches with chopped onion or cream added, hard-boiled eggs, and various samples of Holland's many cheeses.

Certain street foods show a strong Indonesian influence. There are window displays where a version of each dish is shown: one is a *loempia,* an Indonesian spring roll; there is pork sautéed and served with Indonesian sauce; and another is the potato *kroket,* a long fried cylinder of potato puree that is rolled in bread crumbs and may have various other ingredients mixed into the puree, including fried onions, sliced bacon, and even chopped green cabbage.

Sweet pancakes are Holland's version of the French crêpe. *Poffertjes* were once synonymous with the poorer foods of Holland; now they are found everywhere. These tiny yeast pancakes are served with a sprinkling of powdered sugar. Tantalizing doughnuts, freshly fried, are also popular.

36

Poffertjes are tiny pancakes that will be piled on a plate, then covered with butter and powdered sugar.

The city of Gouda, of course, is known for its cheese, and the beautiful old market that is named for it, while Delft is famous for its blue-and-white porcelain. Along the streets of both cities, street-food vendors sell the same fresh wares that make street food in Holland a delight. One traditional sweet not to be missed is the *stroopwafel,* a sandwich made up of two still-warm fried wafers filled with a fresh caramel sauce made of sugar and that justly famous Dutch butter. *Stroopwafels* are sold individually or packaged for consumption at home.

Although mass-market hamburgers and other "junk foods" have also made their appearance on the streets of Holland, it is nice to know that there are still many vendors serving the wonderfully original fresh street food that offers the best kind of "Dutch treat."

Herring is prepared in Delft with
patience and deftness.

Opposite above:
Traditional Dutch caramel wafers are
offered everywhere in Delft.

Opposite below:
A selection of sweet Dutch doughnuts
and rolls draws customers to this stall.

India

Early in the morning, two boys prepare breakfast for their fellow workers in the spice market of Old Delhi.

*T*he concept of "street food" in India is much broader than in many other countries. Food prepared on the street is not always intended for sale, money is not always exchanged. For some people, the street serves as a kitchen—the place where their food is cooked and eaten.

It is early morning at the ancient Curry Bowly spice market in Old Delhi. The street is quiet, and the light has a bluish hue. Most of the spice stalls are still closed. At the edge of the street are rows of rickety carts made of long wooden planks linked to a frame narrow enough to negotiate through the market's tiny alleys. Attached to the frame are two large wooden wheels and two long handles for guiding the cart. Some porters are still sleeping atop a number of these carts, covered with bags to protect them from the morning chill. Others are already up, carefully soaping themselves and then rinsing with cold water near a large metal faucet in a corner.

Moving into a narrow alleyway that departs from the main road thrusts the visitor back in time. A few steps down the lane is a large, square courtyard surrounded by an ancient building that had once been elegant and luxurious. The courtyard is now crowded with small shops stocked with sacks of spices, and so closely packed that there is hardly room inside for even one person. The rising scent from the spices scorches the throat and dilates the nostrils.

Above:
Chapatis are prepared in a Sikh temple for the traditional daily meal that is offered to all who may arrive.

Opposite:
An efficiently folded food stall is carried to a busy street corner.

Youngsters squat in a corner of the alley preparing *chapati,* the most common of Indian breads, for breakfast. One of them kneads a ball of dough with quick motions, obviously experienced in this task. Another young man shapes the dough into little balls and flattens them with a small rolling pin. He deposits the dough onto a hot metal surface atop a three-legged stool beneath which are burning logs, flips it, and—in moments—the hot, crispy *chapati* is ready. He casts the bread, which is covered with brown singe marks from contact with the hot metal plate, onto a pile of previously cooked rounds.

Nearby, a brown lentil stew boils steadily in a small pot. The youngsters spoon the stew onto pieces of *chapati* and sit down to satisfy their hunger. This is one essential kind of Indian street food.

Later, when the market is bustling with activity, the food stalls will come to life. Some will offer that very same breakfast—a type of bread served with a helping of lentil stew. Shoppers, porters, and market mer-

42

chants are among the daily customers. The scene is captivating: Porters, their heads wrapped in scarves, drag sacks of spices along on their narrow wooden carts, their muscles contracting, sweat streaming down their skin. The scarves and the rest of their clothes are a light pink color, and it takes only a moment to discern that the color itself is a residue of the spices they carry on their carts.

As the day progresses, activity at the Curry Bowly Market increases. Yogurt and cheese sellers occupy one section of the market, the same area where ghee (the purified, slowly cooked butter that constitutes the main cooking fat used in Indian cuisine) is sold. Another section is home to the legume and spice merchants. Interspersed throughout the market are the food stalls. Some vendors are mobile, carrying their equipment to the spot they intend to occupy. Each balances on his head a large metal plate brimming with all the ingredients he will need. One shoulder supports a wooden stool that is often attached to a wicker basket used for discarded remnants. After settling down somewhere, each quickly sets out to prepare his dishes. Legumes top the list of ingredients in Indian street food, and lentils are the most common type. Some-

times they are fried until crispy, made into patties, or used as the main ingredient in thick, hot stews. Each dish is differently spiced, and has its own distinct flavor.

Chickpeas are also a common ingredient. Fresh chickpeas soaking in water are piled high in a handsome basket. The chickpeas are a bright green color and the basket is covered with a dark red cloth and adorned with red flowers. This colorful display is a focal point on a busy street.

A chickpea dish is sold on another street corner. A large copper jug narrow at the top rests on a cart, its opening tilted toward the vendor.

Fresh chickpeas are food for the body, while the flowers are for the soul.

He uses a large spoon to scoop out a hot chickpea stew into a dried leaf that has been shaped into a bowl. (Until a few years ago, these stews were served in fresh leaves, and in some regions they still are.) He then sprinkles a mixture of spices into the leaf bowl, which develops a pleasant aroma upon contact with the hot stew.

This spice mixture, known as *garam masala,* has many variations. In each, spices are roasted for several minutes in a dry pan and then ground in a mortar with a pestle until they have been reduced to a fragrant powder. The spice mix varies from region to region, in accordance with the different cooking styles. Many Indian dishes include some form of this mixture. Sometimes food is marinated in it; other times the spice mix is added during the initial stage of cooking—often when the food is being fried—and on still other occasions, it is added during the final stages of preparation.

The successful use of so many diverse spices is more challenging than one might think. It requires a certain culinary wisdom and a light touch. Overseasoning can upset the flavor balance of a dish and ruin its taste. An established culinary tradition and extensive experience are required to create a blend that gives a meal that extra something which can transform it into a notable encounter. The right combination of spices should resonate on the palate in perfect harmony and it is at this point that Indian cuisine comes into its own.

Above:

Food once served on fresh leaves is now offered on a disposable plate made of a dried leaf. This vendor is serving spiced chickpeas.

Left:

Curried lamb being prepared on the street. Chunks of meat are added to the fragrant fried spices.

A cloud of enchanting aromas attracts people to one stall in the market, where a large, smiling vendor stands before a huge copper pot containing garlic, onions, fresh hot peppers, and an intoxicating blend of seasonings—one of the many *garam masala* mixtures. He fries the ingredients slowly in ghee, adds a large amount of thick yogurt and chopped cilantro, and lets the stew cook over a low flame as he stirs the enticing green sauce with evident satisfaction.

At the vendor's side is a large tray covered with pieces of lamb—the meat most widely eaten in India, where Hindu doctrine bans the consumption of beef. He slides the meat into the large pot with measured motions. The meat soaks in the green sauce, absorbing its tangy flavor. This is just one of the many curry dishes so common in Indian cuisine. Customers eat the stew spread on a thin bread, taking pleasure in every bite.

Like curry, yogurt is also a staple in Indian cooking. Not only is it tasty, but it actually has a cooling effect when used in or served with spicy dishes. *Lassi,* one of the most common beverages in India, is made from yogurt and sold on the street everywhere. This drink can be found in many variations—sweet or salty, naturally tart, or

Samosas are filled with a spicy mixture of curried potatoes.

seasoned with saffron. In all its forms, it has an invigorating effect, especially in the sultry weather that is typical of India during most of the year.

For vegetarians, India is a never-ending source of wonderful dishes. Many Indians are vegetarians, whether for religious or health reasons. As a result, vegetarian food in this country is a vital part of the culinary scene. The Indian repertoire includes curried vegetables, fried vegetables, legumes, various chutneys, excellent yogurt dips known as *raitas,* and foremost, an extensive variety of doughy delicacies, breads, and pastries. One notable example is a dumpling known as a *samosa.*

This hot pyramid of dough is stuffed to the brim with cooked potatoes, peas, and seasonings.

In most cities, tandoori ovens are scattered in many locations. Alongside them, young men beat doughy balls on flat surfaces and then attach them to the oven's inner walls, where they bake while other foods are cooked in the oven at the same time. Another delicious form of bread is known as *puri,* a flat piece of dough that expands like a balloon as it is fried. Other tasty breads common to India include the *paratha*—a thin, golden crisp—and the *chapati.* Often, some of these breads are stuffed with a thin layer of vegetables, such as radishes or cauliflower. Bread of some kind is an integral part of almost every Indian meal.

India is a huge country with a vast population. Overpopulation is one of its most serious problems, coupled with the country's continuing difficulties in trying to feed all of its inhabitants adequately. There are many large- and small-scale efforts to address this need, as reflected in

Generous passersby purchase meals for the indigents waiting patiently in front of an outdoor kitchen.

When Muslims break their
Ramadan fast, the streets become
the setting for a grand feast.

one part of Delhi, where about thirty men of various ages sit on the
street across from one of the city's food markets. They are indigents who
have no money for food. Occasionally, a generous passerby will purchase
a meal for one or more of the men, who will receive the food in accordance with a certain established order. A special stall prepares meals for
this purpose. The food is simple, filling, and inexpensive: a potato curry,
two types of lentil dishes, vegetable stew, and two kinds of bread. This
network represents one small, but indispensable, part of the effort to
feed those who cannot afford to feed themselves.

In the older section of Delhi, near the great mosque, most residents are Muslim. The difference is apparent in their dress and lifestyle.
During the month of Ramadan, Muslims fast all day and eat only after
sundown. Once it is dark, food stalls appear on the streets and alleys
throughout the neighborhood and people throng from their homes to
break their fasts.

The last day of Ramadan is marked with a festival of sacrifice
known as Id ul Fitr. Locally made amusement rides crowd the narrow
alleys, among them colorful tin carousels that rumble as they spin, and
improvised Ferris wheels with just four seats in each one. The operator
turns the Ferris wheel with one hand while, with the other, he lifts a
child into a well-worn seat. The children's tiny faces radiate with excite-
ment. The crowd, the commotion, and the noise level can be overwhelming.

Enormous amounts of food are prepared for Id ul Fitr. Doughy snacks are fried in huge pots of boiling oil one-and-a-half meters in diameter. The vendor sits, legs crossed, on an elevated platform near the pot, stirring the oil. He pulls out one of the snacks, gives it a good shake, and deposits it on a perforated metal tray. The excess oil drips down through the holes. A delicious yellow rice seasoned with saffron and other spices cooks in a huge pot at a neighboring stall. The pot is wide at the bottom and narrow on top to prevent the heat from escaping. Another vendor nearby stirs a spicy chutney stew in a large casserole.

Elsewhere, in a large stall, spicy snacks made of lentil dough resembling long, thin laces are arranged invitingly beside red onions and hot chili peppers. The lone voice of a muezzin calling Muslims to prayer chimes out in the background, as the crowd sweeps people along in directions they don't always want to go.

The setting changes as one travels to the south of India. This area was once a Portuguese colony and, since then, the south has been home to a large Christian population and a smaller Jewish community. These

A huge frying pan serves up an enormous amount of food to Muslims pouring out of Old Delhi's great mosque on the last day of Ramadan.

49

two groups co-exist with the Hindus of the region, forming a fascinating human tapestry. The area was once a key juncture in the spice trade, an element that has left its mark on the local cuisine.

As one might expect, in the southwest state of Kerala that borders the sea, fish is widely consumed. Fishing nets brought over by the Chinese hundreds of years ago line the beach near the tiny city of Cochin, where fishermen still comb the seas using an old Chinese method. The device they use is made of long wooden strips connected by ropes and designed like a huge crane. The ends of the rope on the beach side are tied to large stones that act like weights for raising the net from the water. At the other edge of the crane, the one facing the water, four long poles are attached to the four corners of a fishing net so that, together, the poles and the net form a pyramid.

The freshest fish possible, from the ancient Chinese fishing nets of Cochin, go directly into the frying pan.

Opposite above:
Masala dosai, the most popular street food in southern India, is a savory pan bread, filled and prepared in front of the customer.

Opposite below:
An extravagant way of pouring tea served with milk is demonstrated by a vendor on the Cochin beach.

The fishermen, wearing only cloths secured at their waists, lower the net into the water. At a given moment they begin strenuously pulling at the crane, lifting it out of the water, using the stones for support. The net emerges full of quivering fish. One of the fishermen runs along the wooden dock that links the sea to the shore, holding a small net. He leans forward, reaches out, and scoops the fish into a wicker basket.

The fishermen sell their catch at an improvised market on shore. Shoppers can take their fish to little shacks just a few steps from the beach where vendors will roast, fry, or otherwise cook them for just thirty rupees a kilogram. The result is a delicious meal of truly fresh fish direct from the sea to the diner's palate.

Here, too, doughy snacks reign in the streets, but with a different flavor and character. *Masala dosai,* one of the most popular Indian dishes to be found in the West, originated in the Kerala region. The vendor who sells these large, thin pancakes, which are airy and delicious, stands behind a hot metal surface. He lifts a ladle full of white batter from a large container and pours the mixture onto the hot surface, making about twenty pancakes at a time, equal in size and perfectly spaced. He pours a few drops of ghee over each one and, working so swiftly that it is almost impossible to follow his movements, spoons a curried potato filling onto half of each circle of batter. He then folds the other half over, creating something like a sandwich that is golden brown and crispy on the bottom. This dish is eminently delicious, spicy, and perfectly seasoned. The batter is usually made from cooked rice that has been ground up and fermented, or from lentil flour, but there are many other kinds of batter, and each has its own customary filling.

Another common food in the south is known as *vadai,* a kind of dough that is fried like a doughnut and sold everywhere in Kerala. This spicy snack has a hole in the middle and is eaten warm.

Strong tea with milk is the most common beverage in this area, which explains where the British acquired their habit of drinking tea this way. For the British, the tea is part of a cherished rite that can include delicate china mugs, elevated pinkies, and small cucumber sandwiches. Indians have an altogether different ceremony. The tea is prepared in pots at food stalls throughout the area until the milk, which makes up a large part of the beverage, takes on a rich, dark tone. The Indians wave their hands and pour the tea into large glasses, sometimes from a height of more than a meter, but the stream is always swift and accurate. Pouring the tea allows the vendor to show off his skill.

While the presentation of the tea is impressive, one of the most remarkable aspects of Indian cuisine is undoubtedly dessert. No dessert available any-

Juicy fried balls of cooked milk are glazed with a sugar syrup to make a wonderful street sweet.

where in the Far East can even come close to matching the taste and quality of those served in India. They are truly exceptional. For instance, there are juicy brown balls of cooked milk, sweetened, fried, and dipped in syrup, a delicacy that can instantly satisfy anyone's urge for something sweet. Or consider dissolved pistachio balls exuding the gentle aroma of exotic herbs, as well as an assortment of doughy biscuits, fried crisp and dipped in a sugary syrup, all fragrant and delicious.

The dessert-maker sits on a tin canister at a street corner, leaning over a large container of boiling oil. He dips one hand into an improvised batter sack and produces a handful of an orange mixture that the boiling oil transforms into a brown, crispy biscuit. The vendor pulls the biscuit out of the oil with a perforated spoon, gives it one quick shake, and tosses it into another container to soak in a brown-sugar syrup. When the soaking is complete, he adds this delicacy to a huge pile of shiny pastries dripping with sugar. They are hard to resist.

Late at night, life on the streets fades slowly. People begin to take refuge in their homes. Those for whom the street *is* home prepare their families for another night of slumber outdoors.

Only the vendors who sell nuts, baked legumes, and sunflower seeds are still open to serve the last few customers. They sit near their stalls, their merchandise arranged in sections. Their gas lamps emit a yellowish light, causing shadows to dart to and fro, as the visitor contemplates another mysterious scene in the life of this unique land.

Above:
A two-step sweet—from the hot frying pan into the bubbling sugar syrup.

Left:
Vendors selling nuts offer a quick, late-night snack.

Indonesia

A noodle soup vendor near a rice field on Bali.

Chopping spices in a village on Bali. The spices will later be fried and sold as traditional mixed spices.

*O*n the island of Bali, a rich panorama of colorful villages nestles harmoniously against the clear blue sea; the rice fields of verdant green on windblown terraces along the mountain slopes provide a delightful contrast. The people of Bali are mainly farmers who work the land with diligence and devotion, living on the foods they raise. The rice,

Above:
An enticing display of *campur rice* dishes in Jakarta.

Right:
Sweet sauce is poured over a coconut snack served in a banana leaf along the way to a temple on Bali.

vegetables, and fruits of their daily diet are enhanced with crops of coffee beans, cocoa, herbs, and spices—which are so abundant that Bali actually enjoys the nickname, "Island of Spices." Even their cigarettes are laced with cloves. Balinese food is generously spiced as well, producing a complex, aromatic, and thoroughly delightful cuisine.

Dining on the street is a well-established tradition here. Morning and evening meals are generally eaten at home, although in a manner very unlike that familiar to Westerners. The Balinese family does not gather around the table; instead, each person takes his or her own meal—usually white rice, a few vegetables, and some chicken or meat—to a corner, sits down, and eats alone.

Nevertheless, the social structure of the island ensures that people spend much of their time collectively, with their families, and with others in their villages. Each village has one or more *banjars,* a kind of men's club. One is for young bachelors, another for married men. Social and religious community affairs are conducted by the *banjar,* including festive cookouts that can last for hours.

There are few restaurants in Bali; those that exist have cropped up in recent years to serve foreign visitors. But when local residents eat out, they eat on the street. They tend to nibble during the day rather than consume full meals, and snacks are available at a variety of food stalls that sell soup with noodles and meatballs, skewered spicy, glazed chicken roasted over charcoal, fried noodles, or *campur rice.*

Campur rice is without a doubt the most popular dish on Bali. Made of many ingredients, it is sold in special glass-topped stalls. Rows of bowls line the shelves along these stalls, each filled with a different accompaniment to the rice: chicken fried until crispy, meat cooked in various ways, vegetables, all steamed or fried with an array of spices. Alongside is a bowl of fried coconut shavings and another bowl filled with a mixture of finely chopped and deep fried spices. On request, the vendor piles rice onto a big plate, and places a sampling from each bowl around it, sprinkling some spices on top. The rice is scooped up with the fingers, together with some of the meat and vegetables surrounding it.

In Bali, food is intricately linked to the rituals of religious offerings. Many dishes are prepared for the gods, offered to them first, and actually only eaten later—when the food has sadly turned cold. Ghosts also play a role in Balinese cuisine. As is true of so much of Indonesia, Bali is an island surrounded by clear blue sea. Surprisingly, however,

During a spectacular Balinese cremation ceremony, members of a *Gamelan* music group are served fried snacks.

fish is rarely included in the local cuisine, and neither sailing nor swimming is a local sport. This is because the Balinese believe that ghosts and evil spirits dwell in the ocean, so they keep their backs to the sea. The beaches are for foreign visitors.

Indonesia is the largest Muslim country in the world, but on Bali the prevailing religion is Hindu-Balinistic, an offshoot of Hinduism. Because this particular island is thus not part of the Muslim world, Bali is one of the few places in Indonesia where pork is eaten, most commonly in *saté*. The meat is ground into small, spicy balls, skewered, and then grilled over charcoal. *Saté* is eaten directly from the skewer. Occasionally, a morsel of liver or another innard is tucked into the ground meat.

On Java, the largest Indonesian island, *saté* is also one of the most popular street foods, but no pork is served here. *Saté* on Java is made with chicken, beef, fish, or shrimp. It is not ground or chopped, but rather speared onto the skewers in small chunks, flavored with spices and grilled over charcoal until browned. When the meat is ready to be served, it is usually topped with a spicy peanut sauce.

Ayam goreng—a crispy spiced fried chicken—

Above:
Ayam goreng, spicy fried chicken, served at a stand on Java.

Left:
One of Bali's most delectable street foods is minced pork *saté*, grilled and sold at many roadside stalls.

is yet another popular street food in Java. It is eaten with *sambal,* an unusually spicy dip that often accompanies fried dishes here.

Time seems to have stood still in the Javanese city of Yogyakarta. The local architectural style shows strong Dutch influence, and the colonial atmosphere is pervasive. Food stalls line the main street of the city and fill the central square that leads to the sultan's palace. Food vendors light gas lanterns in the evening, creating an inviting glow around their colorful stands.

Here, too, various kinds of *saté* are offered everywhere. Other street foods that are prominent in Yogyakarta include the *martabak,* a fried, stuffed, almost crêpe-like treat made individually on the spot. The *martabak* is fried on a metal plate with a slight dip into which some oil is poured. On request, the vendor breaks off a small portion of white dough to form a thin leaf that he drops gently into the sizzling oil. He immediately pours a beaten egg over the dough and quickly adds some spicy ground beef, finely chopped scallions, and fried spices, even before the dough has browned. In four precise motions, he folds up the edges of

Martabak, a savory fried pancake, is offered at a stand outside the old sultan's palace in Yogyakarta.

the dough, creating an edible stuffed envelope. The bottom continues to rest in the center of the hot oil, where it browns and becomes crisp. The vendor then flips the appealing package over and fries the other side for a moment before serving the perfectly cooked pouch wrapped in brown paper.

Eating alfresco can be an enlightening, enriching experience. We were sitting at the single table of a dilapidated wooden shack "restaurant" one day, behind a glass case where two legs of lamb had been hung, one heavy with meat, the other stripped almost to the bone. Upon receiv-

A noodle soup stand in Yogyakarta. The meatballs, noodles, and other ingredients are attractively displayed in the window.

ing our order, the vendor cut some slices of meat into pieces so small that I thought they would dry out on the grill. He poured a modest amount of thick soy sauce into a bowl, added a few spices and tossed the meat in the mixture. Next, the meat was skewered onto thin bamboo sticks—four or five pieces of meat on each one. The skewers were placed on a charcoal grill, six at a time. As we ate, I asked him about *mie goreng*, or fried noodles, another delectable Javanese specialty. He left the shack and walked out into the night, returning within minutes trailed by a thin wisp of a man pushing a colorful wooden cart stall, complete with wok and fire below. The noodles had arrived.

Now we could watch the noodles being cooked. The noodle vendor poured some oil into the large black wok, spooned in some chopped ginger and garlic, freshly chopped chili peppers and chopped shallots. He picked up a cluster of thin, cool noodles, separated them gently and dropped them into the wok, stirring them with a wooden spoon curved to match the roundness of the wok. The noodles turned brown, emitting a pleasant, slightly scorched aroma. The vendor mixed them quickly, adding salt, pepper, and some thick, dark, slightly sweet soy sauce. He divided the noodles into two bowls, topped them with the ever-present

Nasi goreng, a stir-fried rice dish, shows the Chinese influence on the local cuisine.

fried spices, and served them up with a fork and spoon. As we ate, we savored this delightful experience of both Indonesian food and culture.

A more unusual taste sensation for a Westerner, but very popular here, is *otak otak,* an aromatic blend of minced fish. A fish is stripped of its skin and bones, then ground with a pestle to form a thick paste. Spices, coconut milk, and eggs are added; the resulting mixture is molded into a long cutlet, packed in a banana leaf, and roasted on a charcoal grill. It is a delicate dish, kept from cracking or scorching by its banana-leaf wrapping.

Another Indonesian street snack—gaining in popularity almost everywhere—is the *krupuk,* an airy, crispy mouthful of ground shrimp. And, of course, no visitor should overlook the Indonesian version of fried rice, *nasi goreng.*

The coffee served at coffee stalls all over the island is a far cry from the poor imitation often served in hotels. Indonesian coffee is a strong brew that has its own local flavor, and is sweetened according to the customer's taste. The coffee stall is the Indonesian version of the cafe, with regulars meeting there to socialize, as well as to enjoy a good cup of coffee. As night falls and a purple haze begins to descend over the islands of Indonesia, women move through the shadows on their way to place another offering for the gods at a temple somewhere. On the streets, the pace slows, and the day finally comes to an end.

Above:

In the evening, a street "coffee shop" is a lively meeting place where two or three different snacks are offered.

Below:

A variety of fried snacks available at night during a local festival in Yogyakarta.

Italy

A splash of fine olive oil and a squeeze of lemon juice seasons the delicious boiled octopus slices
available in the Vucciria market.

One of the central markets in Palermo on the island of Sicily, named Vucciria, is a little market that bustles with activity, beginning on one tiny street that opens onto a square and flows down adjoining alleyways.

Here, the sheer abundance of the products on display is a constant delight. Fall is well underway one morning and the light rain descending on the town makes the fresh vegetables look even fresher. The artichokes are tiny and purple—small buds attached to long, thick stems. A woman who looks as if she had just stepped out of a Fellini film slashes the stems with a huge knife, using quick, sharp strokes. She throws them into a pile on the side and keeps the tiny buds. These will be transformed in homes, in restaurants, and at street stalls into delicious dishes made of only the freshest ingredients. All it takes is a little care to avoid ruining what Nature has created. The artichoke buds are boiled quickly and soaked in locally produced olive oil that is rich and tasty. They are then doused with freshly squeezed lemon juice and devoured with unadulterated pleasure.

Another locally available delight is freshly cooked octopus, sold at many food stalls for a pittance. Like the artichokes, the octopus is extremely fresh, having been cooked for a precise amount of time without salt and served on a simple platter topped with olive oil and just-squeezed lemon juice. No wonder people line up for this treat, even early in the morning. Wrapped in their coats, some with baskets full of groceries resting at their feet, they stand at the counter, concentrating upon their slices of octopus. One hand holds the plate as each person eats slowly and with appreciation, before continuing on his or her way.

Occasionally, the vendor leans over a big pot in the back of his improvised stall. Steam billows from the top, exuding a powerful scent of the sea. He uses a big stick to stir the water in which several more large octopus are cooking. Soon, they will also be cut into thick slices, dressed with olive oil and lemon juice and served to the steady stream of eager customers.

Meanwhile, shoppers crowd the market and the continual clamor is testimony to its name. Vendors trumpet their goods in loud, mellifluous voices, producing a cacophony of sounds and rhythms. Surprisingly, they all seem to blend into one cheerful and homogenous melody that trills and echoes along the market's streets and alleyways, following the shoppers as they wend their way home. The vendors punctuate their songs with broad gesticulation, as if inviting everyone passing by to approach their stalls and examine the quality of their goods.

Most of the food stalls are strategically located at the market's entrance or exit, where people can pause for something to eat before or after their shopping. *Frittola* vendors usually position their stalls across from the tiny bars in the market that serve wine or beer. This, too, is no coincidence. One vendor stands alongside his basket, occasionally plunging his hand into a tiny opening among the layers of fabric and producing a handful of assorted cooked meats, chopped and shiny with oil. He mounds the meat into a hot fresh bun to make one of Sicily's most traditional dishes. The meat includes pieces shaved off an animal's bones, legs, parts of the head and the tail. These pieces are smooth, oily, and chewy, cooked for a long time in lard until they become shiny and tender. The meat is very salty and the flavor highly concentrated, which quickly induces a raging thirst. For this very reason, the stalls are located near the bars where people can enjoy a glass of local wine or a cold bottle of beer, after they have feasted on the *frittola*.

Many men crowd these tiny bars during the day, some of them workers at the market who spend their breaks eating, drinking, and chatting with friends over the sound of lively music. Other people stop in after completing their shopping, carrying baskets full of the wonderful local produce. They order espressos, drinking them standing up,

Above:

The simplest meats are cooked for hours and then served as street snacks in Palermo.

Right:

A *frittola* vendor with his cloth-covered pot.

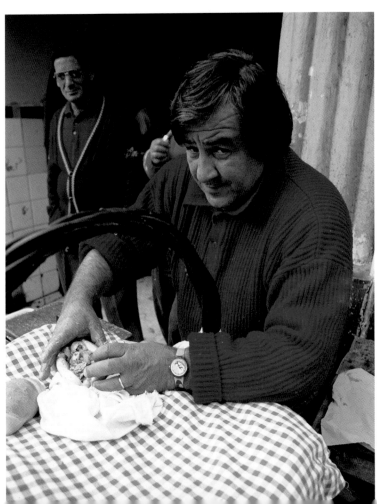

A typical Sicilian sandwich, the *guasteddu,* is spleen fried in lard and served on a bun.

since there are few tables and they are almost always taken. They lean forward, their elbows resting on the bar, nursing a thimbleful of coffee or a glass of wine for a pleasant half-hour.

The *guasteddu* is another popular Sicilian dish common in Palermo. This sandwich is made of slices of spleen fried in lard and served in a fresh roll known as *guasteddu,* hence the name of the sandwich.

With so many shoppers in the market, there is always enough business to go around. Selling fresh food here—and Sicilians are very discriminating when it comes to the quality of their food—is an excellent way to make a living, even when the dishes are simple. The *sfincione* vendor, selling the local version of pizza, wheels his goods through the market on a wooden cart painted a deep blue. Rounds of baked dough are wrapped in plastic to protect them from the rain. One vendor, an amusing young man, maneuvers his cart between the stalls, in and out among the shoppers, bellowing about the quality of his wares. He is hardly exaggerating. The puffy dough is scorched and brittle at the edges, lined with a thin layer of thick, pungent tomato paste made with either fresh or sun-dried tomatoes. The sauce is topped with a sprinkling of *toma,* one of the popular local cheeses, or with some mozzarella. Several drops of local olive oil add to the savory taste of this tart—one of the most appetizing dishes to be found on the island. More elaborate versions are garnished with anchovies, black olives, and other toppings, but the simple pizza is the most popular.

Sun-dried tomatoes are widely used in Sicily. People expose them to the heat of the sun on large wooden platters in backyards, on balconies, or on rooftops. Sicilians generally use the long, thin variety of plum tomato, slicing them in half and leaving them to roast in the hot sun until they are shriveled and dry. The tomatoes are then preserved in jars with olive oil, which renders them tender and tasty. Sun-dried tomatoes are highly concentrated and can easily overpower the flavor of almost any dish, so good cooks use them sparingly.

A number of the food stalls are set somewhat apart from the market's hustle and bustle. The *fritto misto* vendor, for instance, prepares his food in a tiny shop with a wide front window where his customers are served. Behind him is a single electric pot used for deep-frying, while on large trays, stuffed rice

A display of *fritto misto*. This combination of rice, cheese, meat, and vegetables is deep fried until golden.

balls covered with bread crumbs wait their turn to be fried. A large bowl filled with cooked rice is placed strategically in front of him, alongside two smaller bowls full of stuffing mixtures—one made of mixed meat, the other of cheese. He takes a mound of the sticky rice in one hand and uses the other to carve out a dimple, shaping the rice into a bowl with thin walls. He then fills the dimple with some of the stuffing mixtures,

69

seals the opening, rolls the rice into a perfect ball, dips it in bread crumbs and places it on the tray. When the tray is full, he slides fifteen balls into the hot oil. They float to the surface within minutes, their exteriors brown and crusty. This popular street food is known as *arancini*, and is often served with vegetables dipped in batter and fried until they are golden brown. The *fritto misto* trays may also include *panelle*, another one of the island's traditional snacks. These triangular chickpea fritters are among the market's best-sellers.

By early evening, the fruit and vegetable stalls are boarded up and the market is nearly closed. An occasional vendor still mans his stall, but the street-sweepers are already cleaning up.

As the evening progresses, the *stigghioli* vendors make their appearance, slowly erecting their stalls, lighting their charcoal grills, and unpacking their goods. *Stigghioli*, too, is a traditional Sicilian dish, made of lamb intestines woven into long, tight braids. In one variation, the meat is interlaced with green onions. The vendor grills the braid for a long time, dressing it with olive oil and flipping it occasionally until

One of the most popular street foods in Sicily is *pane con panelle*, a bun filled with a bean and chickpea paste, fried in olive oil.

70

it is scorched all over. Smoke billows from the stall as the cooking progresses. Judging by the number of *stigghioli* vendors who set up shop each night, this is an extremely popular dish.

The chestnut vendor nearby isn't doing badly either. He roasts his stock on perforated metal trays over burning coals. The chestnuts crackle as they roast, emitting a tantalizing aroma.

At this hour, the atmosphere on the street is quite festive. Families stroll along the sidewalks dressed in their finery and enjoying the fresh air. Some people will stop for an espresso at one of the bars in the square or to purchase a snack at a street stall. Everyone exchanges greetings, nodding politely. Two men wearing hats strum their guitars and sing traditional Sicilian songs, whose vibrations echo along the tiny alleyways until the last strollers have made their way home. Then, for a few hours, the market will be filled only with quiet shadows.

As evening falls, the regular stalls close in the Vucciria market. Then the night stands open and street foods such as the *stigghioli* are offered.

Roast chicken sandwiches are sold from fully outfitted vans that move to a different market town in Tuscany each day of the week, selling their wares of meats, cheeses, and, of course, *porchetta* sandwiches.

A quick glimpse at this colorful sign indicates that here you might buy a savory *porchetta* sandwich, one of central Italy's most popular street foods.

Opposite:
The smell of roasting chestnuts pervades the winter air near the Fontana di Trevi in Rome.

Mexico

A good place to begin exploring sprawling Mexico City's array of street food is at the edge of the city, in Xochimilco, one of its oldest neighborhoods, an odd collection of square, man-made islands built up over the years on a huge lake.

At the entrance to the area waits a fleet of colorful flat wooden boats, with a picnic table set up along the middle of each one, ready for week-end boating trips along the canals between the islands. The nearby Xochimilco market provides a variety of fresh food products, and street-food vendors offer many familiar, as well as exotic, prepared foods. There are salads, such as those made with cactus and hot chili peppers or fresh green beans, and both fish and meat dishes, including fish tamales and large succulent pork squares that roast slowly on a horizontal grill. Hot pickled peppers and guacamole are

Above:
All the food necessary for a boating feast at Xochimilco can be bought from vendors offering their wares from floating stalls around the lake.

Right:
A vendor sells caramelized apples from his boat on the lake in Xochimilco.

Opposite:
A floating vendor of boiled, then grilled, corn looking for customers in Xochimilco.

75

perennial favorites, as are fresh tortillas from one of the area's many small bakeries. Before the boats depart, excursionists can watch their tables being laden with a sampling of the many different choices, as well as the ever-present bottle of tequila to accompany the open-air feast. A number of boats are actually food stands that sell prepared foods afloat.

Spain influenced Mexico in many ways—culturally, linguistically, and architecturally. But Mexican food has remained largely indigenous, with a culinary tradition that is primarily Aztec or Mayan. Corn serves as the staple of almost every meal, in the form of the tortilla, the taco, or the tamale. These are basic elements in the dishes found everywhere in the streets. Tamale vendors wheel their carts through town, the food kept warm in improvised shells, the variety limited only by the extent of the individual vendor's imagination. The tamale—chopped fish or beef and vegetables rolled in cornmeal dough—is wrapped in a corn husk and cooked until hot and steamy. Corn removed from the cob, and served on a dried corn husk with fresh lime juice and hot chili powder sprinkled over it, is another popular street food. Elsewhere, corn on the cob is served, after having been spread with chili oil and roasted on a grill until the kernels are shiny and brown on the outside, while remaining sweet and juicy inside.

Guacamole, a spicy avocado dip, is sold everywhere on the streets in Mexico.

La Merced is the biggest and busiest of Mexico City's ten markets. Here, vendors stand alongside great round piles of cactus leaves, hacking away at the sharp thorns with huge machetes, selling the leaves for stews and salads. Nearby, great mounds of peppers attest to the spicy qualities of Mexican food. Vendors line the edges of the market, catering to workers and shoppers at all hours of the day. Tortillas made of blue corn are filled with imaginative combinations of chicken, beef, or pork, with hot peppers being the most important ingredient. Stews made of innards—livers, lungs, kidneys, and intestines—are also served from large, steaming pots. Chili con carne, one of Mexico's most exportable dishes, is also popular along the streets of Mexico City. A brown ragout, burning-hot thanks to a substantial number of chili peppers, is served on a plate and spooned up with a tortilla.

Oaxaca offers an interesting contrast to Mexico City. Although the one-story houses are Spanish in feeling, their interior courtyards filled with red and purple bougainvillea and enclosed by brightly colored walls with contrasting windows, the major part of Oaxaca's population is Indian, and they dress in their own lively, traditional garb. Near the main square, the November 21st Food Market is housed in an old warehouse. Each stall offers a single dish, and many may be totally unfamiliar to a foreign visitor.

Oaxaca is famous for its cheese, a large, firm, mozzarella-like white round. For each customer, the Indian woman at the stall will slice off two or three slabs, and cook them over a charcoal grill for about two minutes. When the consistency is just right, she will skillfully transfer the melting mass to a plate containing a generous helping of *salsa verde,* a spicy green sauce made of green tomatoes and large amounts of cilantro.

Another stall will feature a delicious stuffed pepper dish, made with a *poblano* pepper that has been peeled, stuffed, and dipped into a light egg batter, then fried in a deep vat of oil. This dish is accompanied by a mixture of coarse salt, dried ground chilies, and chopped cilantro.

Oaxaca is also well known for its *mole negro,* a dark chocolate sauce that contains peppers, nuts, garlic, and an array of seasonings. It is especially delicious served with chicken and tortillas.

Many traditional charcoal-grilled meats are sold in a dark and smoke-filled alley, where slabs are sliced from large hanging sides of

Grilled yellow and blue corn for sale in the La Merced market in Mexico City.

A girl selling cotton candy in
the main square of Oaxaca.

beef, grilled, and then served on a tortilla. As we were eating, a young woman passed by with a basket of fried grasshoppers, a delicacy of the Oaxaca market. An old-timer complained that they don't taste as good as they once did—before the use of pesticides became widespread.

In the evening, music fills the square, and some promenaders arrive to sit at the stalls and drink tequila, while others enjoy snacks sold at portable stands—coconut sweets, dried fruit snacks, doughnuts, and a colorful round thin pastry that is coated with syrup and dotted with pumpkin seeds—as the Mexican sky turns a burnished black.

Above:
An Indian woman in Oaxaca mixes
the dough for tortillas, using a
centuries-old method.

Right:
A colorful array of sweets tempts the
passerby in Mexico City.

Morocco

Spiced eggs and potato patties are sold in the evening market in Marrakech.

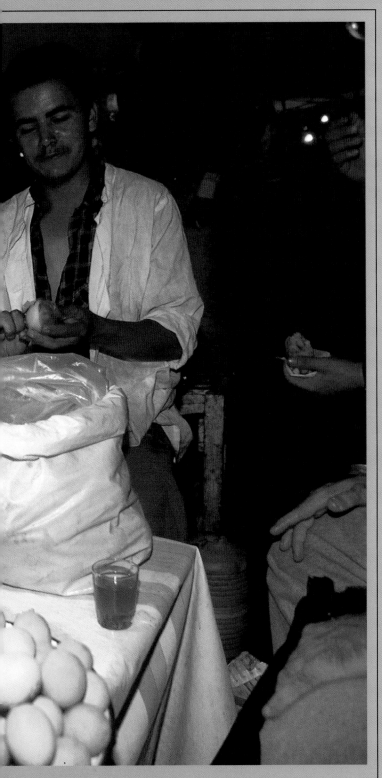

A bluish haze hangs over Djemâa-el-Fna, the central square in Marrakech, as crowds stream into the huge empty space toward evening, just before the sun sets. Almost at once, the square comes to life with an explosion of brilliant colors and clamor. The myriad activities taking place give the square an almost hallucinatory quality. Snake charmers, fire-eaters, tricksters and acrobats, storytellers and medicine men, dancers, singers, and musicians weave their way through the crowds, colorfully dressed and exhibiting their skills with boisterous exuberance. Bellowing vendors add their voices to the singing and the music in chaotic commotion, as a heady blend of intoxicating aromas fills the air. A mysterious force seems to draw crowds toward the center. Most of the people are native, some are foreign visitors, eager to witness a scene that harkens back to the fantasies of a thousand and one Arabian Nights.

It seems as if it could be the entrance to the nether world. Smoke billows up from barbecue grills of the simplest construction: rectangular boxes with covers made of iron bars, filled with glowing coals. Thick metal skewers rest alongside, spiked with cubes of meat, mainly lamb, interlaced with fat from the back of the animal. The meats are grilled slowly over the coals until scorched, and the aroma drifts across the square. As darkness falls, the vendors light yellow-blue gas lamps, setting faces aglow and sending shadows darting everywhere.

The vendors summon the crowds to their stalls, holding out the skewers of meat and intoning in a mellifluous, guttural drawl. It is a temptation difficult to resist, especially when faced with stacks of *merguez*, those delectable lamb sausages wrapped in slightly transparent covers that highlight radiating shades of green and red, hinting at the hidden flavors in the sausage.

The seller grills the sausages for a few minutes, until they are singed with diagonal black stripes. He then stuffs them into a round of fresh bread, adds some sliced fresh onion and hot peppers that have been deep-fried until their skins are all wrinkled, and serves the appetizing package with a triumphant smile. The sausages are plump

Above:
Fried foods of all sorts—stuffed fish, sardines, and potatoes—are very popular in Marrakech.

Right:
At night, a smokey haze surrounds the vendors selling grilled *merguez* sausages.

and spicy, rich and flavorful. The vendor has been especially generous with both red and green hot peppers.

Stuffing the sausages is a dark-eyed young man who works in the rear of the stall. He presses the blended, spiced meat into a long tube, clutching one end and resting the other in a pan of water. He pushes the meat down the tube until it is tightly packed, then ties off the long sausage in measured segments. In minutes, he has produced a shiny heap of fresh *merguez* sausages.

Many different kinds of food in Morocco are prepared over open grills. These popular dishes are eaten everywhere—at home, in restaurants, during holidays, and especially on the street. Vendors grill

Another stand offering a sizzling array of *merguez* sausages.

sausages, chickens marinated in oil and yellow spices, and various kinds of fish. Along the roads between one city and the next, vendors display miniature lambs, headless and without their skins. Next to each one dangles a pair of hooves that identify the particular animal's breed. With a large sharp knife, the vendor slices off a generous portion of the animal's thigh, and cuts it into small cubes on a wooden slab. The cubes are skewered on a metal spit, separated by an occasional onion and pieces of animal fat. From a tiny bowl on the countertop, the vendor takes a pinch of blended spices to sprinkle on the skewer before it goes onto the grill.

In the early afternoon, as the blazing sun beats down and most Moroccans have withdrawn to their homes to rest, the vendors shroud the hanging animals in coverings made of white cloth. The fabric is wet down first, so that it will cling to the body and protect the meat from the harsh rays of the sun. It is a striking spectacle—rows of tiny hanging mummies wrapped in wet cloth, each animal in its own little protective covering.

In a small alley in Casablanca's old city, a little boy has his own small enterprise—grilling corn.

Tagine dishes form another popular and varied group of foods in Moroccan cuisine, named after the crockery in which they are prepared. The *tagine* is a flat clay pot, with a high, cone-shaped matching cover. Because of the unusual shape of this cover, and the fact that it is made of clay, steam accumulates inside, giving the container an oven-like quality. First, the pot is placed over a high flame, and then it is left to simmer for an extended period. This form of slow cooking adds a distinctive dimension to the food, while retaining its fresh flavor.

The ingredients in a *tagine* dish include various combinations: chunks of meat, chicken, or fish, with the addition of vegetables, beans, and spices to flavor the dish. This mixture is cooked slowly over a low flame which produces a rich stew that can serve as a meal in itself.

Above:

At lunchtime, personal *tagines* stand ready to serve at a roadside stall.

Below:

In a small mountain village, a vendor prepares *tagines* of vegetables and grilled lamb kebabs.

Skill and patience are necessary to separate and knead the steamed semolina used to make couscous.

The preparation of a *tagine* differs from region to region, depending upon the nature, season, and type of foodstuffs commonly found there.

Tagine dishes are eaten everywhere, and they can be found at many stalls on the street. Individual portions are often available in tiny, single-serving *tagine* dishes, exquisitely displayed. Their preparation begins around noon, as the vendors pour the ingredients for the stew into the small *tagines,* light the coals underneath them, and allow the stew to simmer for at least an hour. When it is ready, appreciative diners sit on small benches around makeshift tables and eat their fill of the delicious *tagines*.

Stews made of innards are also very popular street foods in Morocco. The thick broth cooks in large enamel bowls, a layer of shiny fat floating on the surface, a combination of hot peppers and cumin imparting a red-yellow hue to the liquid. As the ragout bubbles slowly, it emits a tempting aroma.

Among the most popular street foods is a juicy lamb dish served with chickpeas. This is so delectable and rich that it leaves the mouth sticky long after it has been eaten, recalling the thick gelatin sauce that girdled the meat during long hours of cooking.

Morocco is a country of contrasts, set between desert and sea. One edge of the country thrusts deep into Africa, while the other embraces the Mediterranean and gazes upon Europe. Tribal nomads co-exist within a subtle, sophisticated society. It is a Muslim country, but many Moroccans can trace their roots to ancient mountain tribes. The people are warm and lively, and the tapestry of events in the Djemâa-el-Fna Square in Marrakech heightens this impression.

A sandwich vendor, wearing an ample blue traditional dress, sits on a bench at the edge of the square, her head covered and her face veiled. Only her burning black, luminous eyes are apparent, gazing at potential customers as if inviting each one of them to buy a sandwich.

For each customer, this vendor slices thick, round bread almost in half, stuffs a cooked potato into the opening, then adds a hard-boiled egg and some thinly sliced onion. She sprinkles on some pepper and cumin, finishing the preparation with a generous dollop of coarse, aromatic green olive oil and pushing everything down with a fork. To secure the sandwich, she presses it together, forcing the filling to blend with the bread. So simple and yet so tasty. Four benches surround her, and there is a stool set up amid them, upon which rests a tray filled with fried potato patties, yellow with a cumin topping. A young man sells

A sandwich vendor in Marrakech in her traditional blue dress.

them, calling out to attract hungry customers. He squeezes the juice of a lemon over each pattie and serves it up on a paper square.

Vendors trumpet their goods, sometimes in rhyme. The moment you sit down at a particular stand, you become the personal guest of that

vendor—he will shoo away others who may be vying for your attention. To sit at a stall is to enter an enclave of human relationships, one of feeling and touching. Moroccans will greet someone sitting alongside them with a smile; they will offer a bit of something from their own plates, creating an atmosphere of warmth and shared pleasure.

A meal eaten on a street in Morocco can be a single dish—consumed either standing or sitting—or it may consist of many courses. It is possible to order any number of skewered meats, *merguez* saugages, or animal innards, and the vendor will garnish the plate with an assortment of cooked vegetables: a salad of carrots dressed with lemon, olive oil, and cumin; fried eggplant slices garnished with chopped onions and garlic; zucchini cooked in crushed tomatoes; boiled chickpeas; an onion salad; fried hot peppers; and deep-fried potatoes (a French import). Dishes are always accompanied by a portion of *harissa,* a spicy pepper sauce that is appealing to those with palates to match. In general, most Moroccan dishes are not heavily spiced, but they are usually served with a spicy relish on the side. Many include lemons preserved in salt, a key flavoring that gives Moroccan cuisine a distinct and unmistakable flavor. And there are the olives—green, purple, and black, marinated with lemon and spices, mixed with a hot pepper sauce, or soaked in olive oil. Homemade preparations of olives are served at most street stalls.

Moroccan bread is often homemade, as well. Many families, restaurant owners, and street vendors prepare their own dough, molding it into various shapes and sizes. They carry the unbaked loaves on wooden trays to the neighborhood baker, and return a short time later to collect their freshly baked, golden-brown loaves. The bakers mark the loaves with toothpicks, to distinguish one from another, so that each person may recognize his or her own bread.

Above:
In Casablanca, deep-fried fish are sold alongside the fresh variety.

Opposite:
Deep-fried chili peppers and sliced eggplants are offered in the main square at Marrakech.

There are many different kinds of snacks available on the street in Morocco. One that is widely available is called *sfinge,* shiny, doughnut-like morsels carried on a string like the beads on a necklace, that children often walk around selling. *Sfinges* are always fresh, and usually prepared at a centrally located kiosk. The young vendors pick up a stack and traverse the market, selling their supply quickly, and returning to the kiosk for more.

Another popular street snack is made with snails, cooked in a large bowl and wrapped in a paper cone that can be carried with you as you walk around.

Whenever Moroccans end their meals—whether at home, at a restaurant, or on the street—they do so with traditional mint tea. This is black tea, heavily minted, and sweetened with lots of sugar in the form of rough cubes cut from sugar cones. But mint tea is not reserved for mealtimes, it is served throughout the day and upon every occasion. It is a delightful accompaniment to Moroccan food and a pleasant gesture that embodies the essence of Moroccan hospitality.

Boiled snails are a popular street food in the Casablanca bazaar.

Above:
Afternoon tea is served—very sweet and
strongly flavored with mint.

Right:
Sugar cubes to sweeten Moroccan mint tea
will be cut from this sugar cone.

Peru

Above:
Potatoes being prepared for a special *watias* feast.

Opposite:
A street food vendor sells her wares to the crowd gathered
for the Inty Raimi festival in front of the giant Incan
fortress above Cuzco.

*T*he annual Incan celebration, *Inty Raimi,* held in the ancient city of Cuzco high up in the Andes, is a festive introduction to Peru's street food. On the shortest day of the year, at the Sacsahuamán Fortress, rites are conducted as they were five hundred years ago, with an Incan priest praying fervently for longer days. It is a happy festival, celebrated until dawn on each of its two nights.

Inty Raimi is a major event for the food vendors who set up their portable stalls along the streets. The potato is an Incan gift to the West, and hundreds of varieties can be found here. They are all popular in Peru, where they are served and preserved in many different ways for eating year-round.

At the Inty Raimi festival, the potato plays a special role. The harvest has just ended, and the vast fields around the city (with the snowcapped Andes lying beyond) have been freshly plowed, turning up clumps of rich, dark earth. After the religious ceremony, the colorfully clad celebrants pour into the fields to honor the potato with a *watias* feast, using small ovens that are constructed from mounds of earth. Each family builds a small, igloo-shaped oven, stuffing twigs and branches inside and lighting them. The potatoes are placed in the oven, atop the burning wood, and then a large stick is used to compress the top of the oven down over them. The burning continues inside the oven, the potatoes cook, and after about forty-five minutes, they are removed to be eaten on the

A final stirring of the *chicharrón* before serving. The pork chunks are boiled and then fried in their own fat until crisp and brown.

spot with a sprinkling of salt. They are not for sale, but the generous Peruvians often invite bystanders to share in their potato feast.

The celebration continues. An old Incan woman sits preparing *chicharrón* for sale. A succulent piece of pork is simmered in a deep pot. As the water evaporates, the pork continues to fry in its own fat, becoming a shiny brown. Sliced potatoes are added to the pot to sauté in the pork fat, as well. When the cooking has been completed to her satisfaction, she cuts off a large piece of pork, adds some potatoes and kernels of corn that have also been fried, and presents this delicious combination to the lucky diner.

Corn is a well-established local staple, and the tamale is a popular food item here, as in other Central and South American countries. In Cuzco, the tamale is called a *mite*, and it is both delicate and smaller than those found in most areas. (It comes in a sweet version, as well.)

Another vendor prepares stuffed peppers for frying. Local peppers come in different sizes and colors, as well as varying degrees of sharpness, but this vendor is stuffing a medium-size pepper that is moderately spicy. A strip is cut away from the side, and the pepper is filled with a richly seasoned mixture of rice and vegetables, dipped into a batter, then deep-fried.

During the two-day Inty Raimi festival, various drinks accompany the food: juices, a corn-extract liquor, or one distilled from broad beans, or an alcoholic beverage made from locally grown purple corn, all served up from large clay jugs.

In contrast to the sparkling heights of the mountain villages, Lima is a mixture of extremes: Miraflours, the modern city, and Old Lima, home to street vendors who offer their wares to passersby all day long. Peruvian food has four main sources: the indigenous Indian cuisine, and food introduced by the Spanish, the Chinese, and the Japanese. *Ceviche,* served everywhere along the streets of Lima, is a fish preparation of Japanese origin. The sliced fish is combined with red onion, pepper, fresh chili, cilantro, and plenty of fresh lime juice. After marinating in this mixture for several hours, the fish is ready to be served.

Noodle dishes everywhere in Peru attest to a strong Chinese influ-

Above:
Tamales—cornmeal packed in corn leaves and then steamed until hot and fluffy—are served everywhere on the streets of Cuzco.

Left:
In a Peruvian Sunday market, green peppers are stuffed with cheese and fried.

Above:

An orange juice vendor on the way to a good location for her stand early in the morning.

Left:

In a small Andean village, a homemade alcoholic drink made from corn is sold to the customers at a Sunday market.

ence. Piles of noodles are cooked in a fish or meat broth, seasoned with fresh cilantro, and served with lime wedges. One day, in the Chinese Market of Old Lima, we found a vendor selling the popular *masa morde,* a thick, sweet porridge made of rice and milk. In a second pot, he had prepared a purple-plum marmalade. The porridge was served in a bowl, topped by the very sweet jam, a fitting Peruvian way to indulge the most demanding sweet tooth.

We watched another vendor preparing *parihuela,* a fish soup, using a wok. First, she poured in some water, then a bit of corn extract liquor. As the liquid began to boil, she added a chopped tomato, several cloves of garlic, and some red peppers, finishing with a paste made of chilies and cilantro. She cooked this mixture for a few moments and then added the main ingredients: sliced octopus, a few pieces of fish, some clams, two shrimps, and a cut-up crab. As the soup began to bubble, she added some corn flour to thicken it and served the soup with a handful of lightly fried corn kernels on top.

From Lake Titicaca, a huge lake several miles from La Paz, the capital of Bolivia, come many different kinds of fish that are sold widely in this landlocked country. There are markets that feature only fish as their street food—fried in a batter, or stewed with peppers, onions, and garlic, then served over rice with a flourish.

In Peruvian markets, against a backdrop of spectacular scenery and to the sound of music that evokes the sounds of birds flying high in the mountains and the wind whistling around their tall peaks, the visitor can sample street food that represents the best of the local produce, as well as the skill of those who prepare and serve it as a modern expression of their ancient culture.

Above:
In the morning, chicken noodle soup is a special treat in the Old Lima market.

Below:
Fish and seafood soups with fried kernels of corn are prepared on the spot for customers in Lima.

Thailand

In the evening, assorted spicy meats grilled over charcoal are sold in front of the Bangkok central market.

$\mathcal{E}$*ating on the street in Bangkok is not just* for those watching their wallets. It is an experience that offers a special pleasure, a satisfaction that dining at a conventional restaurant often lacks.

The street food available here differs from one area of the city to the next. In the more affluent neighborhoods—often near office buildings where people are more likely to have deep pockets—the food prepared at the outdoor stalls is more costly, although still quite reasonable by Western standards. One may find huge shrimps still encased in their shells, being grilled over charcoal, well-seasoned with herbs and spices that produce an intoxicating aroma. There are no fresher shrimps anywhere in the world, nor any that are larger, meatier, or more delicious.

Live crabs rest in a tub at the side of the stall, their intimidating claws tied tightly

Aesthetically arranged smoked fish are a major attraction on a street in Bangkok.

99

with string to prevent them from pinching one another, the vendor, or a customer. With quick strokes of the cleaver, the vendor cuts the crab into four pieces, then cracks the shell with a single blow, using the flat part of the cleaver, to make it easier for the customer to pry the shell open and draw out the tender, succulent meat once the crab has been cooked. Smoke rises and a bubbling sound can be heard as the vendor throws the crab pieces into a sizzling wok, adds a pinch of chopped ginger, some green onions, freshly chopped chili peppers, shrimp paste, a handful of chopped lemongrass, garlic, and fresh basil leaves, together with some sugar, a few drops of soy sauce, and a dollop of thick brown fish sauce.

With a light touch and a secure hand, he stirs, shakes, and bounces the wok, sending the ingredients up into circular orbit above the rim of the wok and catching them again as they fall back into the pan. Within minutes, he serves this delectable dish in a plain white bowl to the lucky customer, having produced in short order what is known in Bangkok as "chili crab," one of this city's most popular street foods.

As is true of the food itself, the stalls in Bangkok are both distinctive and diverse. Some are stationary, attached firmly to the ground and hooked up to electric outlets. These stalls generally include a few stools and a counter where the food is displayed, or a number of small folding tables that can turn the stall into a miniature outdoor restaurant. Other stalls are more eclectic, with perhaps a bar, a "display window," a stove, and a grill. At night, they are lit with gas lamps, and the water they use is stored in huge containers. These stalls, usually lined up in a row, have a certain transient quality, as if someone might just grab hold of one and move it someplace else.

There are still other vendors who carry their wares in woven baskets on opposite ends of a bamboo pole, which they balance on their shoulders. One basket usually contains fresh produce, ready for cooking, while the other holds a small stove or a grill, together with a pot or some other container used for steaming.

Thai vendors employ nearly every known cooking technique, incorporating all kinds of ingredients. Food is grilled, stir-fried, deep-fried, steamed, or subjected to long, slow cooking. Among the foodstuffs a visitor will find readily available are fish, vegetables, noodles, rice, chicken, every type of meat, stuffed dumplings, soups, stews, and doughy snacks in various shapes. Most cooking is done quickly, right in front of you, in a burst of colors, tastes, and aromas.

Opposite above:
The Royal Thai family reigns over this cart filled with ice-covered pineapples.

Opposite below:
An amazing variety of grilled meats is on display in one of the many stalls at the weekend market in Bangkok.

Spicy grilled chicken on bamboo skewers is a popular item on the streets in front of the weekend market.

Thai cuisine in its present form is just a few hundred years old. It was originally based upon fish, vegetables, and fruits that grew wild. In time, various regional influences made themselves felt. Chinese immigrants introduced new farming methods that led to organized tillage. They also brought cattle and fowl with them, as well as a variety of cooking techniques. The use of a broad array of spices came from India. Even the various types of chilies, a staple in Thai cuisine, were an import, brought over by European travelers who had discovered them in South America. These new currents became an integral part of the local cuisine, but they did not supplant it. Over the years, all these elements combined to produce a multiform cuisine, a tapestry that has crystallized into something intrinsically Thai.

Many of the country's residents can trace their roots back to China, and the Chinese influence on Thai cuisine is obvious. Some vendors sell food that is recognizably Chinese, while others offer it with local variations. Steamed dumplings stuffed with an abundance of savory fillings are typically Chinese, as are the bronzed ducks that are displayed in the windows of certain stalls.

But China's most substantial contribution to Thai cuisine is undoubtedly the noodle. The large number of stalls where noodles are sold testify to their popularity.

A favorite dish among Thais is a form of noodle soup that differs somewhat from the original Chinese version and comes in almost infinite variations.

Above:
Dumpling soup being offered at a night market in Bangkok. Soup is sold day and night on the streets in Thailand.

Left:
The Chinese influence is apparent in Thai noodle soup.

The stalls where noodle soup is prepared have two openings at their centers that resemble active volcanoes—craters bursting with

Above:
Noodle stand displays often present the picturesque qualities of still-life painting.

Right:
Mieng kum is a typical Thai dish prepared on the spot: shrimp paste, dried shrimp, ground coconut, and chilies, all wrapped and served in a leaf.

steam. One contains boiling water, the other a clear broth. The vendor in each stall has his or her own recipe. The upper half of the stall features bundles of fresh noodles. Each bundle represents one meal. Also on display are leafy vegetables, fresh bean sprouts, chopped green onions, grilled or otherwise cooked cubes of meat, chicken, or fish. The vendor drops the noodles into a small round sieve, clutching its wooden handle tightly. He dips the sieve into the water for a quick boil. While the noodles are cooking, he pours some sesame oil into a wok, then adds a few vegetables and thin strips of meat, followed by a few ladles of hot broth. When the noodles are done, he pulls the sieve out of the boiling water, shaking off any excess. He slides the noodles into a bowl and only then adds the hot soup.

The soup is eaten at tables that surround the stall, each of which has containers of various condiments: crushed hot peppers, spiced vinegar with slices of fresh hot peppers, spiced fish sauce, crushed roasted peanuts, fresh basil leaves, and an assortment of other ingredients sufficient to satisfy anyone's particular palate. The contents of the soup are eaten with chopsticks, while a ceramic (or plastic) spoon is used for the broth. It is a quick, satisfying, and delectable meal.

Mieng kum is a classic Thai dish traditionally served at festive meals, but it can also be found at many food stalls in Bangkok. A delicate woman vendor, a bamboo pole with woven baskets on either end arranged in front of her, sits on a tiny stool. She takes a small, dark green leaf, folds it into a cone, and spoons in

a thick, brown sauce composed mainly of shrimp paste and spices. Inside one of the baskets in front of her is a set of small saucers filled with assorted ingredients: fried coconut chips, tiny hot peppers, miniature dried shrimp, tiny lime slices, crushed roasted peanuts, fresh ginger, finely chopped shallots, and slices of green mango. She drops a pinch of each into the cone-shaped leaf, gives it a final tuck, and seals in all the delicious flavors. The result is a tasty, invigorating snack.

A sweet pomelo salad is another refreshing street food. Segments of the fruit are mixed with chicken and fresh shrimp, and spiced with tangy lime, hot peppers, fried coconut chips, and crushed peanuts. These stimulating cold salads are common in Thailand, with papaya being one of the most popular. This fruit is sliced into thin strips and gently formed into a small crater. Various spices and some fish sauce are added, resulting in a feast for the palate. Some vendors also make a salad of green mango strips mixed with a spicy sauce, chopped shallots, crushed peanuts, and lime.

Sakuna are delicate dumplings, steamed and then filled.

105

Above:
Fishballs in soup provide an attractive nighttime offering in front of Bangkok's central market.

Opposite:
A delightful assortment of meat snacks being fried in another Bangkok night market.

The woman who sells *sakuna* displays remarkable skill. Her stall features two stainless steel chimneys over which a thin cotton cloth is stretched. As steam rises from the chimneys, she pours a white liquid (water mixed with starch) onto the fabric and covers it with a lid. Within minutes, the steam has turned the blend into a thin, translucent dough. She produces a combination of crushed peanuts, dried shrimp, sugar cane and spices, and pours a small amount into the center of the dough. Working quickly, she folds the dough over the mixture, lifts this fragile, transparent dumpling onto a tray alongside a number of others, and douses it with a delicate sauce. The result is a delicious mouthful unlike any other in the world.

Thicker soups made with beef innards or incorporating fish balls are also available at street stalls. These soups are simmered in huge pots and emit a powerful aroma. They are eaten mainly in the evening, and the vendors are adept at accommodating people who are pressed for time. Perhaps you would like to have a bowl of noodle soup with shrimp, but you are in too much of a hurry to sit down and eat it? No problem. The vendor will pour the soup into a plastic bag and secure the top with a rubber band or a piece of string. You can take it to work and eat it there. During lunch hour, when the stalls are besieged by hungry customers, some vendors have bags of soup already prepared and on display at their stands for people to select and continue on their way.

Curry dishes are a prominent feature in Thai cuisine, and many of them are readily available on the street. Vendors can often be seen grinding aromatic spice mixtures with a pestle in an enticing display. They begin with fresh ginger, add shallots, lemongrass, garlic, hot peppers, shrimp paste, and a drop or two of coconut oil, then they beat the mixture lightly. The ingredients are never reduced to a paste, as is common in other cuisines, but instead they are crushed delicately to release their aromas and blend their flavors. This mixture is added to an assortment of excellent ingredients that may include chicken, meat, or fish, also spiced with lime and fresh basil leaves. Coconut milk is then added and the dish is cooked slowly until lunchtime. Appreciative diners enjoy these curry dishes served over a bed of rice.

Eating alfresco provides continuous pleasure throughout Bangkok, day and night, testifying to the city's well-deserved reputation as one of the largest and most appealing open-air restaurants in the world.

Nathan's in Coney Island—famous worldwide for hot dogs and much more.

$\mathcal{M}$*ore than a century ago, Charles* Platman, owner of a beer hall in Coney Island, stuffed a long dachshund-shaped sausage into an equally long roll and introduced one of New York City's most enduring street foods: the hot dog. The sausage itself had originated, together with both its names—frankfurter and hot dog—in the German city of Frankfurt, where the now-famous sausage was originally called a "dachshund."

Platman's clever pairing of sausage and roll caught on and soon became ubiquitous. Nathan's, perhaps the most famous of hot dog vendors (even the Queen of England has eaten a Nathan's hot dog), opened in Coney Island in 1916. Eventually, the hot dog was teamed up with the game of baseball to become an American icon, and the cry of the hot dog vendor became as familiar to Americans as the call to "play ball."

Today, among street foods from almost every cuisine in the world, hot dogs are sold on nearly every street corner in New York City, from permanent stands to wheel-away carts. The customer is offered a variety of trimmings: mustard and sauerkraut, sweet or savory relishes, and ketchup. Luncheon vending begins in the late morning, about eleven o'clock—before that, street food is limited to breakfast items such as coffee, tea, juices, Danish pastries and doughnuts, rolls and bagels (often split and enriched with some butter or cream cheese in the middle).

Above:
Customers wait patiently in line for
a hot dog or knish on Manhattan's
Avenue of the Americas.

Right:
Bagels, rolls, doughnuts, and pastries
are sold with morning coffee and tea.

A striking feature of the lunchtime street scene in New York is the sheer energy and variety of it all. Luncheon carts wheel up to their assigned locations and the tumult begins. On a sunny day on almost every corner of Manhattan, the crowds lining up near the stands or carts have an amazing number of luncheon choices: pizza, hamburgers, soups, tortillas or burritos, falafel or kofta kebabs (spiced rolls of lamb), baked potatoes and french fries, Caribbean jerk chicken or curried goat, a serving of meat loaf atop mashed potatoes, and a seemingly endless array of Chinese and Japanese dishes. The aroma of food as it is being fried or charcoal-grilled wafts out through improvised chimneys and from beneath the colorful awnings that ripple in the breeze. Inviting carts selling fresh fruits are regular fixtures on many street corners where, on the most inclement or most sizzling of days, you can buy oranges, apples, strawberries, a bunch of grapes, or a bag of cherries.

New street foods are always being introduced in New York City. Baked potatoes, straight from the oven, are sold from a locomotive-like stand.

Jackets come off and ties are loosened as Wall Street workers take their lunch break.

Food is carried away to the nearest spot where a seat can be found, to be eaten while chatting with friends and co-workers, as groups gather at the base of a sculpture in the front plaza of an office building, around a fountain, or perch on benches in the pocket parks that abound throughout the city. After jackets have been discarded, ties loosened, and paper bags opened, the relaxed enjoyment of an alfresco lunch is evident everywhere.

On sunny days in New York, lunchtime activity abounds everywhere in the parks. In Washington Square, the chess players and soloists are out amid the skateboarders, gymnasts, and joggers. On those days

112

when the Union Square Market is in full swing, luncheon foods can be purchased and taken away to enjoy in the pleasant park nearby. Central Park is also alive with noontime activities. Vendors are continually busy selling ice cream and pretzels, as well as hot dogs and falafel.

The melting pot that is New York has produced a new variety of street foods that can be baffling to the neophyte: cross-cultural foods. (In fancy restaurants, this kind of cooking is often referred to as "fusion cuisine.") In more down-to-earth locales, the adventurous diner can find any number of imaginative combinations of ingredients. The knish, for example, is available in many forms today—one food stall in Spanish

A refreshing summer treat in Harlem—a sweet syrup is poured over shaved ice and served in a plastic cup.

113

Harlem offers "chili knishes," a version that might raise an eyebrow or two in Eastern Europe, where the knish originated.

Many South American dishes are also sold in the same area. Alongside the chili knish is the *chicharrón,* a crispy piece of fried pork. Another vendor sells ice shaved from a large block and piled into a plastic cup. The buyer selects one of an array of brightly colored syrups, which is poured over the ice, and *voilà:* a refreshing flavored ice to lower the temperature on the hottest day.

During the spring, summer, and fall, there are outdoor food festivals and street fairs all over New York City, where the variety of tempting treats ranges from sausage and pepper sandwiches to curry dishes, from crullers to crêpes, and almost everything else in between.

Chinese street food available on Canal Street and along the narrow streets of Chinatown is particularly varied. Nestled among the souvenir

A wide variety of Chinese food is offered from a small stand in Chinatown: spring rolls, crispy fried chicken wings, salads, and stir-fried noodles.

shops and those that offer an astounding array of Asian goods, are stalls selling golden-brown spring rolls stuffed with a delicate mixture of bean sprouts and vegetables, or rice dough stuffed with diced shrimp and vegetables. One can even buy pyramids of seasoned sticky rice, wrapped in a bamboo leaf and steamed, that do not differ substantially from similar delights you would find in China.

Although most of the moveable carts are wheeled home for the night, this does not mean that the street-food carnival ends at sundown. At more permanent windows all over town, you can order pizza, hamburgers, fried chicken, french fries, pretzels, or bagels and lox, fresh lemonade, or an egg cream (made with syrup, seltzer water, and milk, but never with eggs or cream), or nibble on freshly roasted chestnuts, or on peanuts at a stand from which rises the irresistible aroma of simmering caramel. New York is a summer—and winter—street-food festival that never dims its lights and never closes down.

The sweet scent of roasted peanuts with a caramel coating attracts a crowd near the Guggenheim Museum in Soho.

115

Uzbekistan

*O*n the hottest days of summer, the temperature in Bukhara can sometimes exceed 45 degrees Celsius (over 110 degrees Fahrenheit). This city is a desert oasis, acting as a repository for those icy waters that result when the snow melts on the surrounding mountaintops. In times gone by, Bukhara was awash with natural pools and fountains that spouted streams of water high into the air. The desert winds scattered pellets of water throughout the city, creating the cooling effect of a natural air conditioner. Frogs filled the pools and storks (which fed on the frogs)

Above:

Manty, before steaming. The technique is Chinese in origin, but the ingredients and flavors are distinctly local.

Opposite:

It is traditionally a man's job to prepare the *pulau,* a stew made of lamb, rice, onions, and carrots.

The legacy of Mongolian occupation includes horse meat and lamb fat sausages.

built their nests on top of the city's minarets—those tall towers from which the muezzin would call the people to prayer.

Over the years, some of the pools became sources of disease, and most of them were destroyed. Eventually, there were hardly any fountains that remained intact, so the frogs and the storks abandoned the city. Only the outline of an occasional nest atop a minaret gives testimony today to that enchanted period in the city's history.

For centuries, Bukhara was one of the most important transit points along the Silk Road. Long convoys of camels laden with silks and other goods made their way slowly across China and on to Europe. As they made their way through the desert, traders would stop at one of the city's many taverns to rest, enjoy the surrounding beauty, conduct a little business, and harness their energies for the remainder of the journey. The city was conquered several times by various armies, and destroyed more than once. Its strategic location made Bukhara a coveted prize.

The fact that this city was a central and important junction is evident in many spheres. The culture includes Chinese, Mongolian, Tatar, Persian, and Muslim influences. All of these currents merged over the years into a single rich culture, a delicate and colorful fabric not unlike those variegated silks transported in the ancient convoys.

Such a cultural integration is clearly manifested in the local cuisine. The Mongols left behind their horse salami, the Chinese contributed a variety of steamed dumplings, the Muslim legacy is apparent in the profusion of lamb dishes, and the Persians taught the local residents how to season their dishes with fresh herbs.

During several decades of this century, Bukhara—like other cities in the area—was subjected to an authoritarian and dogmatic communist rule. All religious and indigenous cultural activity was suppressed in an effort to create a uniform communist society. Many forms of the local architecture were allowed to decay and crumble. Only in recent years has the independent Republic of Uzbekistan begun the process of restoration with the help of various international endowments. National pride is also being restored as many historic and religious monuments are refurbished and preserved.

It is in this spirit that the city's four ancient markets have been renovated. These magnificent stone structures are covered with domed roofs in a twisted web of colored stones. The stones are embedded in the roofs at different angles, resulting in an exotic web of light and shadow. The arches within the markets have been reconstructed by local craftsmen, catapulting these locales back to the days of their former glory. Today, however, the markets are still only partially active.

Bukhara's busiest market is actually located within one of the city's newer structures, and it is bursting with life and color. The most notable thing about the market today is its cleanliness. As colorful and charming as they may be, many markets in other countries are not always as clean as they could be. But this is not true in Uzbekistan. The market in Bukhara, like those in Samarkand and Tashkent, is tidy, orderly, and carefully partitioned. Vegetables, fresh fruit, dried fruit, herbs and spices, breads and other baked goods, milk products, fresh meat—each category is sold in its own section of the market. Processed meat products are sold in a separate area where salami sausages made from horse meat hang on hooks along the corridors. At the market's periphery vendors sell tiny treasures and ornaments—jewelry from Turkmenistan, colorful silken fabrics, and embroidered wall hangings, known as *suzani,* an indigenous Uzbek tradition.

Freshly made bread being sold in the market at Samarkand.

119

Today, one of the best markets in Uzbekistan can be found in Samarkand, located in a huge courtyard surrounded on three sides by buildings, and on the fourth, by a mosque named after Bibi Khunum, the wife of one of the city's ancient rulers. This roofed market is also divided into sections and endowed with a healthy assortment of goods. The roof in the bread section is supported by wooden pillars etched with traditional carvings. The aroma here is intoxicating. Colorfully dressed women vendors stand behind wooden or stone counters displaying their goods: round loaves of bread with slightly depressed centers, adorned with symmetric designs.

Traditional breads, decorated in the middle, are offered in Bukhara's market.

In Uzbekistan, commercial bread hardly exists. Bread is baked at home in round stone or clay ovens. Nearly every home has two kitchens, one for cooking and the other to house the oven. The unbaked dough is inserted through an opening at the top or along the side and is pressed against the hot oven's inside wall as the fire burns at the base of the kiln. Slowly, the bread becomes crisp and brown along the wall of the oven, while the top of the loaf remains soft and shiny. This is the traditional bread found everywhere in Uzbekistan and every city has its own variation.

Bread is breakfast's main component and goes very well with a special sour cream known as *kaimak*. Early in the morning, several young women stand alongside a tiny wooden stall on one of the streets of Samarkand. *Kaimak* fills several simple clay bowls lined up on the stall. The cream is very thick, almost solid, shiny and white as ivory. Next to the stall stands a woman with a cart full of round, sweet-smelling loaves of bread covered with fabric to keep them fresh and warm.

Some older men step forward to buy bread and *kaimak*. They tear off a piece of the loaf with their fingers, dip the bread into the cream, raise it in a twisted motion to avoid spilling even a drop, and enjoy this delicious breakfast where they stand.

On cold winter days, the *kaimak* is a basic ingredient in *shir chai*, a strong green tea cooked with the sour cream and salt. The tea is served in a bowl together with pieces of bread that soak up all the flavors. This

An afternoon of repose in a popular *chai-khana*, in Bukhara.

is a custom left behind by the Mongols during one of their periods of occupation.

Breakfast is not always eaten standing up, however, and many meals are consumed at the teahouses that are common in Uzbekistan. Known as *chai-khana*, these teahouses are prevalent along the roads and in town squares. One such *chai-khana* is located on a road leading from the marketplace in Samarkand to the meat market. It is situated along the sidewalk, covered with a high roof that is supported by shabby wooden pillars. Wide wooden beds line the walls of the teahouse, covered with thick blankets and pillows. Perched on each bed is a small rectangular table. Customers kick off their shoes, climb up onto the bed, and stretch out in comfort. The teahouse is filled with food stalls offering an array of dishes.

The tea is brought out first, a hot green tea served in a round clay pot. It is poured into mugs with huge apertures in an atmosphere reminiscent of teatime in China.

On a warm, sunny day you can spend a pleasant hour in a *chai-khana*, drinking green tea, sampling the many edible delights available and enjoying the theater of life: the lively parade of colorful people, the daily exchanges, the commerce, the meetings and partings, the continuous hustle and bustle. The women's heads are wrapped in scarves, the men's are topped with square hats, their backs covered with woven capes.

Samsa is one of the tastiest and most popular foods sold on the street. These rolls, made of a soft, pleasant dough, are stuffed with a mixture of onions, lamb, and lamb fat. They are spiced with *zira*, delicate cumin granules common to the local cuisine. The *samsa* is baked in the same oven as the loaves of bread, pressed to the wall of the kiln until it becomes crisp and brown.

At the busy market in Tashkent we witnessed a curious scene. Two people were preparing *samsa*, quickly stuffing the dough with the meat mixture, adding pieces of lamb fat and then rolling up their sleeves as they stood on stools facing one another on either side of the oven's opening. Next to each of these bakers was a platter of unbaked *samsa*, arranged in rows. One baker palmed a *samsa*, bent over, and thrust his hand into the clay oven, pressing the dough to one of the walls. As he straightened up to take another *samsa* from his platter, the other baker seized the opportunity to thrust his own savory pastry into the oven. This dance repeated itself, one baker bending over while the other straightened up, choreographed in fluid harmony like a well-performed *pas de deux*. They followed the same technique in removing the baked *samsa* from the oven, coordinating their rhythmic motions perfectly. Within minutes, they were standing at the front of their stall, selling the hot, fragrant *samsa* fresh from the oven.

Above:
Tea is prepared in old samovars in a *chai-khana* on the outskirts of Tashkent.

Opposite:
Samsa will bake slowly in the oven as customers wait patiently.

Two bakers will alternate as they put their *samsas* in the oven with well-coordinated movements.

This market in Tashkent is always bustling with activity. Every item imaginable is sold here. In the "Men's Department," dozens of vendors sit on the floor, alongside their merchandise, crowded shoulder to shoulder and leaving only a narrow lane for the customers passing by. At noon, a man suddenly appears carrying a pot filled with noodles and lamb. The vendors sit in long lines as they eat, their bowls filled with the steaming stew.

In another corner of the market, a young man slices onions on a rectangular cutting board. He holds a large, slightly curved knife as he slices vigorously with measured, rhythmic motions. Onions are a staple of the local cuisine and Uzbekis have a technique for taking the bite out of them. They pile the chopped onions into a large colander, sprinkle them with a healthy dose of salt and let them sit for an hour while the bitter juices slowly ooze out. Then they squeeze out the remainder of those juices to create a kinder, gentler onion.

124

Above:
Vendors on their lunch break in the
Tashkent market.

Left:
Chopping onions in a special box reserved
for that purpose. The onions will then be
mixed with meat for the *samsa* stuffing.

In the center of the market, a vendor tends to a large pot, its rounded bottom resting on an open flame. The pot contains *pulau*—rice brimming with long carrot strips, onions, and *zira*. A large chunk of enticing brown lamb garnishes the rice, topped by a piece of lamb fat that keeps everything warm and moist. (Lamb fat is used in place of oil in many Uzbeki dishes.) Being the son of Bukhari parents, I remember *pulau* as a special dish served at festive meals. I was surprised to discover that, in Uzbekistan, *pulau* is eaten everywhere: at home, on special occasions, and on the street, as well. This dish has several variations, sometimes cooked with chickpeas, black raisins, or quinces, and sometimes topped with sliced meat. Preparing *pulau* is usually a man's job. Women can be seen in the market peeling and slicing carrots into the long, thin strips that are added to the rice.

Pulau is usually eaten with the fingers—it's a tradition. The food is spooned into a bowl and placed at the center of the table in the *chai-khana*. Diners scoop up clumps of rice with their fingers and propel them into their mouths. Proper etiquette requires that the food should never touch any part of the hand beyond the fingers' first joints.

The city of Bukhara has its own special version of this dish known as *chalti pulau*. *Chalti* means "small bag" in Uzbek. Bukhara residents cook the rice for this dish in a bag made of linen or cotton, adding a cup of freshly chopped coriander leaves for every cup of rice. Chopped

Shredded yellow and red carrots have been pre-cut for use in the *pulau*.

lamb's kidney and liver are thrown into the bag, together with selected seasonings. The bag is tied—loosely, to allow the rice to expand—and cooked in simmering water.

Cooking the rice in this bag prevents it from swelling to its utmost and gives it a distinct texture. When the cooking is completed and the bag is untied, the unforgettable aroma of lamb and coriander rises from the dark green rice.

Another popular street food is *manty*. This delicate doughy dumpling is made from very thin dough stuffed with a mixture of lamb and onions. The dough is folded neatly and cooked in a steamer for thirty minutes. The Chinese influence is unmistakable; this is the local variant on dim sum. The shape of the dumpling is similar to the Chinese version, the technique of preparation is identical, but the ingredients and flavors are uniquely Uzbeki.

In a tiny alcove at the edge of the *chai-khana* a woman stands before a table, clutching a rolling pin. She is preparing *manty*. The dough is very thin, nearly transparent, and its edges spill over the ends of the table. When she is satisfied with the dimensions of the dough, she wraps its edge around the rolling pin and folds it back and forth into the shape of an accordion, each pleat being about fifteen centimeters

The first stage of preparing *manty*. Later, a generous amount of minced meat and onions will be added to a thin layer of the dough.

Above:

In the last stage of preparing *manty,* the dough is gently folded over the filling before being steamed.

Right:

Green peppers stuffed with rice and meat are ready in the Tashkent market.

wide. She then slices the accordion-shaped dough into strips of approximately the same width. Each strip is stretched out and sliced into equal squares. She drops a healthy portion of meat into the center of each square and folds it neatly into a handsome dumpling.

Once they are ready to be cooked, the dumplings are arranged on round, three-legged platters made of perforated metal. The platters are stacked one on top of the other, their tiny legs separating one dish from the next. This tower is placed inside a huge pot with boiling water at its base. Steam fills the interior and cooks the dumplings, which will later be basted with oil and served warm.

At the market in Tashkent, women outfitted in colorful scarves sit behind large metal bowls full of *manty* dumplings filled with various stuffings. Some of the dumplings are covered with different dressings. The women are adorned with gold jewelry and exotic makeup. A black pencil mark links their eyebrows in accordance with the local style. They smile at their customers, revealing gold teeth. They offer an assortment of dumplings, including the *dushpara*, which are cooked in a thick, meaty stew and seasoned with a distinctive sour flavoring. The *dushpara* is also of Chinese derivation, being a variation on the wonton, but the flavor is indigenous and quite wonderful.

Shoppers can enjoy a substantial variety of fresh fruits at the markets in Bukhara, Tashkent, and Samarkand, such as sweet and juicy figs, pomegranates with ruby red seeds, apricots, and melons (including watermelons). The fruits and vegetables sold in these markets have been grown traditionally, as was common everywhere before food engineers and geneticists became involved in farming. The flavors are natural and savory. An appealing selection of dried fruits and snacks is also available in these markets, including dried chickpeas and roasted apricot pits.

When you have finished a meal in the *chai-khana,* you can lean back on your couch and abandon yourself to the local music. You may find yourself transported back to the legendary days of Nasser a-Din and the intriguing lives of Bukhara's emirs. At Bukhara's Lobby House on the bank of one of the ancient pools, a *chai-khana* stands in the shade of an old mulberry tree with thick branches. The neighbors of this teahouse include a seminary and a mosque, both of which are painted in shades of turquoise and green. Perhaps some day a vestige of the grandeur of days gone by will return to this land, together with the frogs and the storks.

Recipes

China: Chinese Noodle Soup

Serves 4

INGREDIENTS:

8 dried Chinese black mushrooms

½ pound egg noodles

1 tablespoon plus 4 teaspoons sesame oil

4 cups chicken broth

About 1 inch fresh gingerroot, shredded

2 tablespoons soy sauce

Salt and freshly ground white pepper

½ cup fresh soybean sprouts

½ cup cooked chicken, shredded

Bok Choy or mustard greens

1 green onion, finely chopped

1. Soak the mushrooms in warm water for ½ hour. Squeeze the mushrooms dry, remove and discard the stems. Slice the caps into thin strips.

2. Cook the noodles in a large amount of salted water until they are just soft. Drain and rinse under tap water. Place in a bowl and add 1 tablespoon of the sesame oil. Coat well.

3. Separate the noodles into four portions. Pour the chicken broth into a pot and add the mushrooms, gingerroot and soy sauce. Bring to a boil and cook over a low flame for 10 minutes. Add salt and white pepper to taste.

4. Place 1 teaspoon of the sesame oil into each of four soup bowls, add a small bunch of soybean sprouts and some of the chicken and greens to each bowl. Add the boiling soup, and sprinkle the green onion over the top to serve.

Throughout China, delicious and quickly prepared noodle soups are made in a seemingly endless variety of methods and flavors.

France: Sugar and Lemon Crêpes

Serves 4–6

INGREDIENTS:

1 cup flour

1 tablespoon sugar

Pinch of cinnamon

1 tablespoon Muscat wine

2 eggs

1 ²/₃ cups milk

Unsalted butter, for frying

Juice of 2 lemons

Powdered sugar, for sprinkling

1. Mix the flour, sugar, cinnamon, and Muscat wine in a bowl. Beat the eggs with the milk and add to the dry ingredients, stirring until the mixture is completely smooth. Chill for several hours.

2. Melt some butter in a non-stick crêpe pan, and pour in about 1 generous tablespoon of the batter. Whirl it quickly around to ensure that the batter covers the bottom of the pan. As the crêpe firms, flip it over with a spatula and cook for a few seconds on the other side. While it is still in the pan, douse the crêpe with a bit of melted butter and a squeeze of lemon juice. Sprinkle with sugar, fold into quarters, and slip off onto a plate for serving.

The skillful art of preparing a delicate crêpe
in Paris is displayed outdoors.

good grating of nutmeg, and salt and pepper to taste. Mix well and allow to cool for an hour.

4. Shape the potato mixture into sausage shapes about 3 inches long by 1 inch in diameter. Roll them in the breadcrumbs and refrigerate for an hour. While still cold, deep-fry in hot oil until they are browned. Place on a paper towel to drain and serve hot.

India: Lamb Curry

Serves 4–6

INGREDIENTS:
1 teaspoon mustard seeds
2 teaspoons coriander seeds
3 pods of cardamom seeds, cracked
1 tablespoon chopped fresh fenugreek seeds
1/2 cup clarified butter
2 hot chili peppers, finely chopped
4 garlic cloves, finely chopped
1 large onion, finely chopped
About 1 inch fresh gingerroot, finely chopped
2 pounds lamb shank, in 1 1/2-inch cubes
2 cups thick yogurt
Salt and freshly ground black pepper
1/2 cup chopped fresh coriander (cilantro)

1. Place the mustard seeds, coriander seeds, cracked cardamom, and fenugreek seeds in a small, dry frying pan. Cook over a medium flame for 3 minutes, stirring all the while. Remove from the heat, place in a mortar, and crush.

2. Melt the butter in a small frying pan, and add the chopped chili peppers, the garlic, onion and gingerroot. Stir-fry for 3 minutes, then add the lamb and crushed roasted spices. Fry for another five minutes.

3. Add the yogurt, salt and pepper to taste, and the coriander. Lower the flame, and simmer for about 1 1/2 hours.

Convenient, inexpensive, and freshly prepared snacks are widely available from automatic machines in Amsterdam.

Holland: Potato Kroket

Serves 4–6

INGREDIENTS:
1 large onion, finely chopped
2 pounds potatoes, peeled and cubed
4 eggs
1/2 cup flour
Fresh nutmeg, grated
Salt and freshly ground black pepper
1 cup breadcrumbs
Vegetable oil, for frying

1. Fry the onion until it is golden brown. Set aside.

2. Boil the potatoes in salted water until they are soft. Drain and put them back into the dry pot over a medium flame, shaking the pot until the potatoes are completely dry, 3 or 4 minutes.

3. Mash the potatoes into a smooth paste. Add the eggs, the fried onion, the flour, a

Large pots are used to cook rice with saffron, a popular street food in Old Delhi.

Indonesia: Skewered Chicken Saté

Serves 4

INGREDIENTS:

1 pound chicken breast, in ½-inch cubes

FOR THE MARINADE:

3 tablespoons sweet soy sauce
3 tablespoons peanut oil
2 shallots, finely chopped
Salt and freshly ground black pepper

FOR THE SAUCE:

3 tablespoons peanut oil
2 garlic cloves, finely chopped
2 shallots, finely chopped
About 1 inch gingerroot, finely chopped
1 small hot chili pepper, finely chopped
1 teaspoon brown sugar
1½ cups coconut milk
Salt and freshly ground black pepper
1 tablespoon lime juice
1 green onion, finely chopped

1. In a large bowl, mix the ingredients for the marinade. Put in the cubed chicken, making sure each piece is well covered, and allow to marinate for at least 1 hour.

2. Skewer the chicken pieces onto bamboo skewers.

3. To prepare the sauce: Heat the peanut oil in a pan, and add the garlic, shallots, gingerroot, chili pepper, and brown sugar. Stir fry for 3 minutes. Add the coconut milk, salt and pepper to taste, bring to a boil, lower the flame, and simmer for 10 minutes. Add the lime juice, and stir again.

4. Grill the skewered chicken over hot coals for 2 minutes on each side, basting with the marinade.

5. To serve, place the grilled chicken on a plate, add the sauce, and top with chopped green onion.

This *saté* vendor has chosen a strategic spot near the entrance to Yogyakarta's main market.

Italy: Sicilian Pizza

Serves 4–6

INGREDIENTS:

½ ounce active dry yeast

½ teaspoon sugar

About ¾ cup lukewarm water

1 pound flour

About ½ cup olive oil

2 teaspoons salt

1 pound plum tomatoes, peeled, seeded, chopped, and left in a colander to drain while the dough is prepared

Salt and freshly ground black pepper

12 anchovy fillets, washed under cold running water

24 black olives, pitted and chopped

2 tablespoons chopped fresh oregano

¾ cup grated Pecorino or Parmesan cheese

1. Place the yeast in a bowl and add the sugar and the water. Mix well, and allow to rest for ½ hour. Add the flour, 4 tablespoons of the olive oil and the salt, and combine well until the mixture becomes a kneadable dough. If it is too sticky, add more flour. If the water is not absorbed completely, add a little more lukewarm water. With floured hands, knead the dough until it becomes shiny and elastic, about 10 minutes.

2. For two pizzas, divide the dough into two balls. Cover each with a dry cloth and allow the dough to rest and rise in a warm spot for at least 1 hour.

3. Preheat the oven to 450 degrees F. Roll out each ball into a large round of not more than ¼-inch thickness, and place on a cookie sheet or pizza pan. Brush each round with some of the olive oil, and spread the tomatoes over the dough. Add salt and pepper to taste, and lay the anchovies decoratively on top of the tomatoes. Sprinkle with the chopped olives, the fresh oregano, and the grated cheese. Brush again with olive oil and place in the preheated oven for about 20 minutes, or until the pizza is crisp. Serve hot.

Outdoors in Palermo, this Pizza Siciliana provides a bright and cheerful note.

Mexico: Cheese-Filled Spicy Peppers

Serves 6

INGREDIENTS:

6 large poblano peppers
Vegetable oil
¾ pound Oaxaca cheese or a firm
mozzarella
2 eggs
3 tablespoons flour
Salt and freshly ground black pepper
Vegetable oil for deep-frying

Indian women gather near a self-service grill in Oaxaca's covered market.

1. Rub the peppers with a bit of vegetable oil, and blacken the skins either in a hot oven for 10 minutes, or over a flame. Peel and cool. Make one slit lengthwise, and gently remove the seeds.

2. Divide the cheese into six equal pieces. Stuff a piece into each pepper through the slit.

3. Separate the eggs and beat the whites until stiff. Gently beat the yolks and fold them into the whites. Add the flour, salt and pepper to taste, and mix gently.

4. Holding each pepper by its stem, dip it into the batter and deep-fry in hot oil until golden. Serve hot.

Morocco: Lamb Kebabs with Pine Nuts

Serves 6

INGREDIENTS:

2 pounds ground lamb

3 garlic cloves, crushed

1 large onion, finely chopped

5 tablespoons olive oil

1 cup chopped parsley leaves

2 tablespoons chopped mint leaves

1 tablespoon cumin seeds

Salt and freshly ground black pepper to taste

½ cup chopped pine nuts

1. Prepare a charcoal grill. Place all the ingredients in a large bowl and mix well.

2. From the mixture, form oval meatballs of about 2 inches in diameter. Roast on the hot coals for 3 to 4 minutes on each side or until the kebabs are well browned and crispy.

Buying a snack in Marrakech may involve some high-spirited bargaining.

Peru: Ceviche

Serves 4–6

INGREDIENTS:

1 pound fillet of fresh white sea fish (bass, grouper, red snapper, etc.), sliced into 1-inch cubes

1 red onion, coarsely chopped

1 red chili pepper, diced

½ cup chopped coriander (cilantro)

½ cup fresh lime juice

3 tablespoons olive oil

Salt and freshly ground white pepper

1. Mix all the ingredients in a large bowl and refrigerate for 3 to 4 hours. The fish will have marinated well in the lime juice and requires no cooking. Serve chilled as a first course.

Ceviche—raw, marinated fish—is a popular street food in Lima's old district.

If someone's in a hurry, take-away meals in plastic bags are available from street vendors all over Bangkok.

Thailand: Chili Crabs

Serves 4

INGREDIENTS:

8 fresh crabs

4 tablespoons corn oil

4 garlic cloves, finely chopped

3 shallots, finely chopped

About 1 inch fresh gingerroot, finely chopped

2 small hot red peppers, chopped

The white of 1 stalk lemongrass, finely chopped

1 tablespoon sugar

1 teaspoon ground turmeric

4 tablespoons soy sauce

3 tablespoons lime juice

Salt and freshly ground black pepper

4 tablespoons chopped fresh coriander (cilantro)

2 green onions, sliced diagonally into strips

1. Clean the crabs well, and cut them in half lengthwise. Crack the shell of the claws.

2. Heat the corn oil in a large wok, and add the garlic, shallots, gingerroot, peppers, and lemongrass. Stir-fry for 2 minutes.

3. Add the crabs and stir-fry for another 5 minutes or until the crabs turn red. Add the sugar and turmeric, and stir for another minute.

4. Add the soy sauce, the lime juice, and ¼ cup of water. Season to taste with salt and freshly ground pepper and stir-fry for another 5 minutes.

5. Sprinkle the green onions on top and serve.

U.S.A.: Falafel

Serves 4–6

INGREDIENTS:

½ *pound chickpeas, soaked overnight*

½ *cup chopped parsley leaves*

½ *cup chopped coriander (cilantro)*

1 large onion, coarsely chopped

4 garlic cloves

1 green chili pepper

1 teaspoon ground cumin

Salt and freshly ground black pepper

1 teaspoon baking soda

Vegetable oil, for frying

1. Drain the chickpeas and grind them together with the parsley, cilantro, onion, garlic, and chili pepper. Place in a bowl, and add the cumin, salt and pepper to taste, and the baking soda. Cover and refrigerate for at least 1 hour.

2. From the batter, make small balls about 2 inches in diameter. Flatten slightly.

3. The falafel can either be deep-fried or sautéed in less oil on one side, then the other. They should be cooked until well-browned.

Buying kebabs on Fifth Avenue in New York City.

139

Uzbekistan: Samsa

Serves 20

INGREDIENTS:

FOR THE DOUGH:

1 pound flour

1 tablespoon active dry yeast

1 teaspoon sugar

2 teaspoons salt

¾ cup vegetable oil

1 egg, beaten, for glazing

FOR THE FILLING:

1 pound lamb, chopped

3 large onions, chopped

1 tablespoon salt

2 tablespoons cumin seeds (whole)

Salt and freshly ground black pepper

1. Combine all the ingredients for the dough. Then add enough water to create a smooth, but not sticky, dough. Knead for about 10 minutes, cover with a dry clean cloth, and allow to sit for another 10 minutes.

2. Mix all the ingredients for the filling in a bowl, and reserve a little more than a heaping teaspoonful for each *samsa*.

3. Divide the dough into small balls, and flatten to a diameter of about 5 inches. Place a heaping teaspoonful of filling in the center of each *samsa*. Fold the edges over the filling and seal. Flatten the stuffed dough, and place it on a lightly oiled baking sheet with the seam side down.

4. Preheat the oven to 350 degrees F. Glaze the *samsas* with the beaten egg and bake for another 20 minutes, or until golden brown.

Samsas, buns filled with minced lamb and onions (shown here just before they go into the oven) are one of the most popular street foods in Uzbekistan.

Acknowledgments

Films: Fujichrome Velvia; Kodakchrome EPJ

Cameras and lenses: Nikon

Laboratory Services: Studio M, Tel Aviv

Travel Consultant: Geographical Tours—Neot Hakikar

*T*o *our families who could not join us in our travels, whom we had to leave behind—Nelli's wife, Udit, and* children, Lior, Mika, and Nadav; Aharoni's wife, Gigi, and children, Tamara, Rachel, and Uri—we extend our thanks from the bottom of our hearts. They are with us everywhere we go.

We cannot adequately express our thanks to our friend and agent, Beth Elon, who struggled with us more than ever to make this book materialize; for her consulting, translating, and, most of all, for her encouragement.

Special thanks go to Mosh Savir, manager of Geographical Tours—Neot Hakikar, who helped so much in getting us to the most exotic places. And thanks to Shula and Oded Modan, for their support and belief in our books all these years. Not least, we would like to thank Yehudith Levison, who worked so hard to free our aching backs each time we returned from faraway places. Thanks, also, to Mimi Sheraton, whose generous and professional advice we have always found so helpful.

Our thanks also go to friends and professionals who worked with us: Mosh Gilad, Itay Scoropa, Meir Carmon, Moshe Hertzhaim, Jacob Hadar, Liora and Dick Codor, Roni Rubinstein, Liu Shi Jun, Piero Galvagni, Gita Bhalla, Moshe Mena, George Zohar, Malka Percal, and Michael Ginor.

But most of all we are grateful to the many anonymous street food vendors, street cooks, and local patrons whom we met while working on this book. Thanks to all those who extended their hospitality, gave us tidbits of information, shared their food and recipes with us, and most of all, made the world seem friendly, hospitable, and wonderfully tasty wherever we went. It is they who have made this book worth doing.

Nelli Sheffer and Israel Aharoni

Bibliography

Bayless, Rick and Bayless, Deann Green. *Authentic Mexican: Regional Cooking from the Heart of Mexico.* New York: William Morrow, 1987.

Grant, Rose. *Street Food.* Freedom, California: The Crossing Press, 1988.

Halvorsen, Francine. *The Food and Cooking of China: An Exploration of Chinese Cuisine in the Provinces and Cities of China, Hong Kong and Taiwan.* New York: John Wiley & Sons, 1996.

Marks, Copeland. *The Exotic Kitchens of Indonesia.* New York: M. Evans & Co., Inc., 1994.

Mayson, James. *Street Food from Around the World.* Sydney: Simon & Schuster, Australia, 1997.

McDermott, Nancie. *Real Thai: The Best of Thailand's Regional Cooking.* San Francisco: Chronicle Books, 1992.

Poladitmontri, Panurat and Lew, Judy. *Thailand: The Beautiful Cookbook.* San Francisco: Collins Publications, 1992.

Wolfert, Paula. *Couscous and Other Good Food from Morocco.* New York: Harper & Row, 1987.

Yan, Martin. *Martin Yan's Culinary Journey through China.* San Francisco: KQED, 1995.

Zaslavsky, Nancy. *A Cook's Tour of Mexico: Authentic Recipes from the Country's Best Open-Air Markets, City Fondas, and Home Kitchens.* New York: St. Martin's Press, 1995.

Illustration Credits

FRONT COVER: Even in winter, ice cream is enjoyed outdoors in Paris.

BACK COVER: *China.* Charcoal-roasted yams are sold from an oven on wheels in Beijing.
Holland. A large sign advertises the fried potatoes at a stand in Gaude.
Indonesia. A spice mixture being prepared on the street in Yogyakarta.
India. Fried chickpea-based snacks are offered by a vendor in Old Delhi.
Italy. Slicing *porchetta* for sandwiches during a village festival in Tuscany.
Uzbekistan. Lamb and tomato stew simmering outdoors in a Tashkent market.
Thailand. Deep-fried snacks for sale on a busy street in Bangkok.
Peru. A typical market lunch—noodle soup with pork and corn.

PAGE 1: A woman carefully observes the duck eggs being cooked on a street in Shanghai.

PAGES 2–3: Caramelized apples being sold from a boat on the lake in Xochimilco, Mexico.

PAGES 4–5: In New Delhi, this porridge made of semolina and pistachios is very popular.

Index

All page numbers in italics refer to illustrations

Amsterdam (Holland), *32*, 33–36, *34*, *35*, *132*
Andes. *See* Cuzco (Peru)
Apples, caramelized (Mexico), *2–3*, 75
Apples, sugared (China), 22, *23*
Arancini, 69–70
Ayam goreng, *59*, 59–60

Baba, *17*, 17–19
Bagels, 109, *110*
Baguettes, 26–28, *27*, *28*, 30
Baked potatoes, *111*
Bali (Indonesia), *8*, *54–56*, 55–59, *58–59*
Bangkok (Thailand), *10*, *98–100*, *99–101*, *103*, 104–6, *106*, *107*, *138*
Banjar (men's club), 57
Bao zi, *18*, 19
Beijing (China), 23
Brittany (France), 25–26
Broodjes, 33, *34*
Brooklyn. *See* Coney Island (USA)
Bukhara (Uzbekistan), 117–19, *120–21*, 126–29

Campur rice, *56*, 57
Cancale (France), 25
    See also Brittany (France)
Caramel wafers, *38*
Caramelized apples, *2–3*, 75
Casablanca (Morocco), *84*, 88, *90*
Ceviche, 95, *137*, 137
Chai-khana (teahouse), *120–22*, *121–22*, 126, *127–29*
Chalti pulau, 126–27
    See also Pulau
Chapatis, *42*, 47
Charcuteries (France), 26
Cheese-Filled Spicy Peppers, 136
Chestnuts, *30–31*, 31, 71, *73*, 115
Chicharrón, *10*, 94, *94*, 114
Chicken noodle soup, 97
Chickpea stew, 44
Chili con carne, 76
Chili Crabs, 99–101, *138*
Chili knish, 113–14

Chili peppers, fried, *88*, *89*
Chinatown (USA), *114*, 114–15
Chinese Noodle Soup, 130
    See also Noodle soup, China
Chong, *12–13*, 13
Cochin (India), 50, *50*, *51*
Coffee, 62, *63*
Coney Island (USA), *10–11*, *108–9*, 109
Congee, 19
Corn, grilled, *74*, *84*
Corn on the cob, 76
Cotton candy, 35, *35*, 78
Couscous, *86*
Crêpes, 25–26, *26*, 131, *131*
    See also galettes
Curried lamb, *45*, 46, 132
Curry, 46
Curry Bowly spice market (India), 41–43, 46
Cuzco (Peru), *92*, 93–95, *95*

Delft (Holland), *7*, *38*, *39*, 39
Delhi (India), 48
    See also Old Delhi (India)
Djemâa-el-Fna market (Morocco), 81–83, 86–88, *89*
    See also Marrakech (Morocco)
Dried squid, 22
Duck, royal Beijing, 20
Duck, Yunnan, 20, *20*, *21*
Dumpling soup, *103*
Dushpara, 129

Eels, smoked, 33–34
Egg cream, 115
Eggplant, fried, 88, *89*

Falafel, 111, 139
Fish, fried, *88*
Fishballs, 106, *106*
Fritto misto, *69*, 69–70
Frittola, 66, *67*
Fusion cuisine (USA), 113

Galettes, 26
    See also crêpes
Gamelan music group (Indonesia), 58
Garam masala, 44, 46
Ghee, 43, 51

Gouda (Holland), 39
Grasshoppers, fried, 78
Grilled corn, *74*, *84*
Guacamole, 75–76, *76*
Guasteddu, *68*, 68

Harissa, 88
Harlem (USA), *113*
Herring, *7*, 32, 33, 39
Horse salami, 118, *118*, 119
Hot and spicy dumplings, *6*
Hot dogs, 35–36, 109, *110*

Ice cream, 30, *31*
Id ul Fitr festival (India), 48–49, *49*
Inty Raimi festival (Peru), *92*, 93–95

Jakarta (Indonesia), *56*
Java (Indonesia), 59–62
Jenever, 33

Kaimak, 120
Kerala (India), 50–51
    See also Cochin (India)
Khwo, 20–22
Knish, *110*, 113–14
Kofta kebabs, 111, *139*
Kroket, Potato, 36, *132*
Krupuk, 62
Kunming (China), 19–20, *20*
    See also Yunnan (China)

La Merced market (Mexico City), 76, 77
Lake Titicaca (Peru), 97
Lamb Curry, *45*, 46, 132
Lamb Kebabs, 84, *85*, 137
Lamb Kebabs with Pine Nuts, 137
Lamb sausage, *118*
    See also Merguez
Lamb with chickpeas, 86
Lassi, 46
Laughing cookies, 22
Lentil stew, 42, *43*
Lima (Peru), 95–97, *97*, *137*
Loempia, 36

Mango salad, 105
Manhattan. *See* New York City (USA)

Manty, *117, 127,* 127–29, *128*
Marrakech (Morocco), *80–82,* 81–83, *86–88, 87, 89, 137*
Martabak, *60,* 60–61
Masa morde, 97
Masala dosai, 50–51, *51*
Merguez, *82,* 82–83, *83,* 88
Mexico City, *8–9, 74, 75,* 75–76, *77, 78*
Mie goreng, 61
Mieng kum, *104,* 104–5
Mint tea, 90, *91*
Mite, *95,* 95
Mole negro, 77

Nasi goreng, 62, *62*
Nathan's (hot dog vendor), *108–9,* 109
New Delhi, *4–5*
    See also Delhi; Old Delhi
New York City (USA), 109–15, *110–15, 139*
Nice (France), *6*
Noodle soup
    China, *14–16,* 14–17, 130, *130*
    Indonesia, *54–55,* 57, *61,* 61–62
    Peru, 95–97, *97*
    Thailand, *103,* 103–4, 106
Noodle stand (Thailand), *104*
Noodles, spiced, 61–62
November 21st Food Market (Oaxaca), 77

Oaxaca (Mexico), 76–78, *78, 79, 136*
Octopus, *64–65,* 65–66
Old Delhi (India), *40–41,* 41–43, 46, *133*
Olives, 88
Onions, 124, *125*
Orange juice, 95, *96*
Otak otak, 62
Oysters, *24,* 25, *25,* 31

Palermo (Italy), *64–65,* 65–71, *67, 68, 71, 135*
Pane con panelle, *70*
Panelle, *70,* 70
Papaya salad, 105
Paratha, 47
Parihuela, 97
Paris (France), *24,* 25, 26–31, *27–31*
Patat frites, *33, 34,* 34–35
Peppers, stuffed
    Mexico, 77, 136
    Peru, *95,* 95

Uzbekistan, *128*
Pineapples, *100*
Pistachio balls, 52
Platman, Charles, 109
Poblano (pepper), 77
Poffertjes, 36, *37*
Pomelo salad, 105
Porchetta, *9,* 72
Potato Kroket, 36, 132
Potato patties, *80–81,* 87–88
Pulau, *116, 126,* 126
    See also Chalti pulau
Puri, 47

Raitas, 46
Ramadan, *48,* 48–49, *49*
Rome (Italy), *73*
Royal Beijing duck, 20

Sacsahuamán Fortress. *See* Cuzco (Peru)
Sakuna, *105,* 106
Salsa verde, 77
Samarkand (Uzbekistan), *119,* 119–22, 129
Sambal, 60
Samosas, *46,* 46–47
Samsa, 122, *122–25,* 140, *140*
Saté, *8, 58–59,* 59, 60, 134, *134*
Saté sauce, 35
Scheveningen (Holland), 33
Sfincione, 68–69
Sfinge, 90
Shanghai (China), *1, 18,* 19
Shir chai, 120–21
Shorpa, *11*
Sicilian Pizza, *135,* 135
Sicily (Italy). *See* Palermo (Italy)
Sikh temple (India), *42*
Skewered Chicken Saté, 134
Smoked eels, 33–34
Smoked fish, *99*
Snails, 90, *90*
Soho (USA), *115*
Soka, *6*
Spiced chickpeas, 45
Spiced eggs, *80–81*
Spiced noodles, 61–62
Spicy grilled chicken, *102*
Steak Tartare, 36
Steamed chicken (Yunnan-style), 19–20, *20–21*
Stigghioli, 70–71, *71*

Stroopwafel, 39
Stubbe herring stand (Holland), *32*
Stuffed peppers
    Mexico, 77, 136
    Peru, *95,* 95
    Uzbekistan, *128*
Sugar and Lemon Crêpes, 131
Sugar cone, *91*
Sugared apples, 22, *23*
Suzani (wall hanging), 119
Szechwan (China), 20–22, *22*
Szechwan hot pot, *22*

Tacos, *8–9,* 76
Tagines, *84–85,* 84–86
Tamales, 75, 76
    See also Mite
Tandoori ovens, 47
Tashkent (Uzbekistan), *11,* 119, *122,* 122–26, *125, 128,* 129
Tea
    India, 51, *51*
    Morocco, 90, *91*
    Uzbekistan, 120–22, *122*
    See also Chai-khana (teahouse)
Tequila, 76, 78
Toma, 68–69
Tortillas, *8–9,* 76, 78
Tuscany (Italy), *72*

Vadai, 51
Vucciria market (Italy), *64–65,* 65–71, *71*
    See also Palermo (Italy)

Watias, *93,* 93–94

Xi'an (China), 17
Xochimilco (Mexico), *2–3, 74, 75,* 75–76

Yin-Yang principle, 22
Yogurt, 43, 46
Yogyakarta (Indonesia), *60,* 60–62, *61, 63, 134*
Yunnan (China), *17,* 17–20, *20–21*
Yunnan duck, *20,* 20, *21*

Zira, 122, 126